Grass Chapels

MERCER UNIVERSITY PRESS

Endowed by

TOM WATSON BROWN
and
THE WATSON-BROWN FOUNDATION, INC.

Grass Chapels

New & Selected Poems

WILLIAM WRIGHT

MERCER UNIVERSITY PRESS
Macon, Georgia
2021

MUP/ P629

© 2021 by Mercer University Press
Published by Mercer University Press
1501 Mercer University Drive
Macon, Georgia 31207
All rights reserved

25 24 23 22 21   5 4 3 2 1

Books published by Mercer University Press are printed on acid-free paper
that meets the requirements of the American National Standard for
Information Sciences—Permanence of Paper for Printed Library Materials.

Printed and bound in the United States.

This book is set in Adobe Caslon Pro.

Cover/jacket design by Burt&Burt.

ISBN   978-0-88146-799-4
Cataloging-in-Publication Data is available from the Library of Congress

Acknowledgments

ℰ

Thanks to the following editors of presses and journals who believed in and published my work. Some of these poems were published in volumes and journals in slightly different forms:

NEW POEMS

A Literary Field Guide to Southern Appalachia (The University of Georgia Press); *Birmingham Poetry Review; Eighth Bridge; Grist; Louisiana Literature; McNeese Review; Oxford American; Prairie Schooner; Rock & Sling; Southern Humanities Review; Story South; Terrain.org.*

POEMS FROM PREVIOUS VOLUMES:

AGNI; Asheville Poetry Review; Beloit Poetry Journal; Birmingham Poetry Review; Broad River Review; Colorado Review; Crab Orchard Review; Devil's Lake; Epoch; Five Points; Floyd County Moonshine; Flycatcher; FREE; Greensboro Review; Grist; Kenyon Review; Louisiana Literature; Midwest Quarterly Review; New Orleans Review; North American Review; One; Pacific Review; Poet Lore; Rattle; Red Owl; San Pedro River Review; Shenandoah; Smartish Pace; Snake Nation Review; Southern Poetry Review; Story South; Tar River Poetry; Terrain.org; Texas Review.

POEMS IN
Specter Mountain (Mercer University Press, 2018)
Creeks of the Upper South (Jacar Press and Unicorn Press, 2016)
Tree Heresies (Mercer University Press, 2015)
Xylem & Heartwood (Finishing Line Press, 2013)
Night Field Anecdote (Louisiana Literature Press, 2011)
Dark Orchard (Texas Review Press, 2005)

Thanks to *Blue Horse Press* for publishing *April Creatures,* from which the poem with the same title has been taken.

Thanks to Jacar Press and Unicorn Press for publishing *Creeks of the Upper South.*

Thanks to *Texas Review Press* for publishing *Dark Orchard* and *Bledsoe,* from which sections of the book have been taken.

Thanks to Jesse Graves and Amy Wright, who collaborated with me with their own beautiful poems in the volumes *Specter Mountain* and *Creeks of the Upper South,* respectively.

Thanks to Marc, Marsha, Jenny, Mary Beth, and Heather at Mercer University Press for believing in my work.

A final thanks to artist Emoni Viruet, whose painting was created for the cover of this volume.

for my mother, father, and sister,

and for cherished friends,

Paul Chesser, Brandon Wicks, Martin Sheehan,
James Howell, and Dan Morris

Contents

Preface

William Wright invokes the Muses. He writes visionary poems in the old sense, conjuring images from the deep subconscious—maybe the collective, maybe only his own. The poems sort and sift through the past, through near and distant memories, yet they feel alive and attuned to the present and mindful of the future. Wright's poems brim with the detailed specificity of his close observation of plants, animals, rocks, flowers in fields, water maneuvering between creek banks. He studies large-scale motifs (the cosmos), the micro-world (atomic and subatomic realities), and the complexities of all life. One encounters an almost microscopic examination of insects, like the yellow jacket and the cicada. Accurate recording alone, however, does not create memorable poems—details must be encompassed by a conceptual framework, an interrelating vision that adds depth and significance to the imagery. William Blake may have seen the world in this way, or Emily Dickinson adrift in her rooms, or Hart Crane late at night and in his cups. "Sing to me," Wright seems to beckon, "sing to me, o Muse, of spirits in high hidden coves and beneath the marshy shallows." The poems in *Grass Chapels* peer into the dark corners and empty halls of old barns, where the only life is small and trying to keep hidden. Spiders and moths, mice and the owls and foxes that hunt them all have a home here. This work offers ruin and rebirth in near-equal measure, and when rebirth is not possible remembrance must suffice.

The first set of poems I recall reading by William Wright included "Trumpet Creeper," which would appear in his second full-length collection, *Night Field Anecdote*. In the opening stanza, I encountered the phrase "Lacertilian armies" and reached for my trusted *American Heritage* dictionary. I kept reading and felt increasingly thrilled by the ambition of the language and the scope of the long and multi-faceted poem. When I came to the lines "fields of ducts, white worms, smokestacks— / a trillion trillion cellular divinities," I sensed I was reading a poet informed by both hard scientific learning and alchemy. Next I read "Blonde Mare, Iredell County, North Carolina, 1870–1896," and was stunned by the tenderness of imagining the yoked hardship experienced by both the horse and its owners. The concluding lines of the poem show their final union more than a century later, "all knitted by death's / twine, your crux not lost but heaved by creek / and meadow, sluiced through the blowing manes of trees."

Lyricism is the primary mode in Wright's poetry, but many poems are driven by characters and their narratives. The selections from *Bledsoe* give the deepest immersion into a fictional world where disability and strained family ties bleed into a kind of violence normally associated with true crime drama. In later poems like "The Milk Witch," from *Tree Heresies*, Wright moves beyond folklore into the realm of folk horror, a genre more often discussed in film studies than literature. The image of "the season's rain / locked behind her smiling eyes" reminds us why we fear what happens in the dark, and why we suspect unnatural forces at work when crops fail, and cows run dry. Anyone who reads of the furrow plowed by the blonde mare, or of the shrouded conjuring of the milk witch, will recognize the fine and distinctive thread William Wright has stitched into the flag of American poetry.

I hope readers will pursue *Grass Chapels* straight through and then go back and read it again in reverse. They will see the growth of the poet's mind, how certain themes were planted early and bloom into fullness throughout. The language of botany and geology are present from the beginning, and the longing for deep and familial connection with the past. The earliest poems in the book, from *Dark Orchard*, may lack the formal or technical sophistication of the new poems, but they possess an undeniable brilliance in figuration and imagery. Poems such as "Dreaming of My Parents" reveals Wright's early desire to connect with places of origin and to commemorate the womb and the nest of our upbringing. When Robert Morgan says, "*Bledsoe* reads like a poem by Cormac McCarthy," he pays highest praise to both the stylistic intensity and the conceptual architecture of the book. To have all these poems together in one volume, and to be able to follow the arc from the beginning to the present, is a gift to readers of poetry, and Mercer University Press should be gratefully acknowledged for recognizing the importance of this work.

Can readers know poets through their work? Who is William Wright? I really should be able to answer, as he has been my closest working companion for more than a dozen years. We wrote a book of poems together and have co-edited three volumes of *The Southern Poetry Anthology* series. We have given readings, taught workshops, made "road trips" together, and been part of the same writing group with Dan Morris and James Clinton Howell for a decade. The person *Will* is just as encyclopedic in his knowledge and interests as the speaker of these poems, but he is also funnier. A typical phone conversation with Will might last an hour or two and range from making a list of favorite American poems since 1970 to how to repair a mechanical wristwatch, from the medical issues of our parents to fractals, astrophysics, and quantum mechanics. Will is a video game aficionado, and built his own computer once from scratch, a devoted enthusiast of J. S. Bach's music and surrealist visual art, and a student of cosmology and consciousness. He loves languages and has translated the Austrian poet Georg Trakl, among others, into English. The last book he recommended to me wasn't some little-known poetry volume, but *Parable of the Sower* by Octavia Butler (I loved it, just as he predicted). When I try to connect the threads of all Will has read and watched and listened to, I feel like Jonathan Livingston Lowes furiously tracing the sources of Coleridge's imagination in *The Road to Xanadu*. I know it is an impossible journey, yet what an adventure!

Wright is a younger poet today than either Robert Frost or Wallace Stevens when they published their first volumes. Despite all that these poems have accomplished, a reader anticipates what might lie ahead. In a comment for his 2013 chapbook, *Xylem & Heartwood*, I wrote, "William Wright is the young American poet most likely to discover a new way to frame the deep paradoxes of life and language shown before by Coleridge, by Rilke, and by James Wright." As I read his new poems, I feel more certain of this claim than ever. Lines such as:

> so that nights
> when I can't sleep,
> I can ride out
>
> those creatures'
> compound melodies,
> their one and only hymn.

from the poem "Anodyne" offer proof of the deepening well of his inspiration. William Wright invokes the Muses. They sing.

Jesse Graves
Johnson City, Tennessee, 2019

New Poems

&

Boyhood Trapped between Water and Blood

1.

A boy, I knew nothing of the copperhead's fangs,
swam with them most summers, sank with their faint mint smell
and blue-lit ripple flames of their bodies in creek water—

Kestrels of light
lunged through the water surface and flattened into one great trellis
of sun, every contour of the creek bed
branded in a fire that wove
                                its shape into shapelessness.

Salamanders and crawdads never bothered me,
nor the ticks that teemed on every branch—

                                I was alone
in that chapel of water and wind.

I lived in a yellow house smothered in leaf-shadow
and would dream at night of the creek, clear
as the smell of wood smoke
on a winter dusk blown with stars,
                                even as June rains
engraved the water
with meaning, forever blurred by the sudsy iron that
                                turned water to blood.

My eyes itched with a grief
that was mine and not mine—

                                every night, every night.

North into woods, just out of view,
leaned a rotten three-walled shack
with no roof and the words "die nigger" inscribed

in blood on the west wall—the letters
flanked in blood-red swastikas,

                    a shade of crimson

like the dace that darted in the creek's oxbows;
and there were still signs
of a struggle: scraps of a green T-shirt,
a broken window toothed   in the same blood,
the shattered pane like an eye
blinded,   never storm-cleansed,
                       never burned away.

2.

A boy, I carried sun-drunken notions
of time as song, the crispness
of fall and its subtle rumor—

I did not know why the wind
stirred some father-witted guilt
in me, and as I jumped
from one side of the ditch
to the other again and again,

I could not evade visions
of a man taken by a horde of others
and dragged through
briars and the indifference
of deerberry and resurrection fern—

I knew even then, a boy,
that the man was being forced through
the final door for nothing
more than pigmentation,
and that the only sound he made
were the gasps of air the men

4

kicked out of him
as he lay fading in silence,
his last possession.

And there in the bramble still lay his clothes.
And there on the jagged stone lay the vision of his head.

3.

A boy, I craved design,
a structure through which I came to
understand or escape

words that followed me
like the sound of footfalls
in the leaf-litter just behind actual passage.

Some nights in spring the song thrush
bore out its brash and beautiful music,
as if the world had torn
and revealed an answer,

as if something more had pursued
me and kindled my insomnia
with a plea.

4.

Once a black boy named Seneca
ran with me down the road
and his family waved at us
and shouted encouragements.

We leaned headlong into our running
until breathless,
reckless through the moths

and the distant orchard light

and the moon-curve against
the back of my grandparents'
home where a lamp flicked
on and glowed as we passed.

That same night my grandmother
yanked me in and belted me
until I bled,
screaming the scriptures
until I could weep them back—

my crime the mere nearness
to a "nigger boy," the "tacky" fact
that we were both fierce with joy.

    5.

Eastward, heaps of goat bones dotted
a baseball field overgrown in sicklepod,
                  and every dusk for months
Seneca and I met to sift

through those mythic shapes, to stare
into the eye sockets of many skulls
as if they might rouse in us some memory
of another time, another creature,
to elude the heat and stifle

of that place, scalded with resentments
extravagant as the trees' canopy,
the woods between my house
and the other world always nightfall,
                  unbroken shadow.

Faith

I believe in ghosts, for I have seen
the face of God in the culled body
of a fox scoured clean in a winter field.

A raven's body pasture-hollowed,
its wings and throat borne away
by ants, owls, its eyes flowered

under dusk's purple veil.
I believe in souls, for I have witnessed
the high nests of wasps in the wind-stung

elms of early fall thrive through winter,
shedding brain lanterns burning deep, cold.
I have seen the flexion

of a mud-struck catfish
spring itself back into pond water
gone blood-red, just after rain—

and I have swum through testaments
of sorghum, honeysuckle, shinleaf.
The moss-ridden brick, a silo's silhouette—this

downwardness compels trust in the worlds
behind this one, scriptures carved deep
in grainy light of broken sheds, broken days,

where joy is loneliness, and whether
rust or iris, wound or star, the mind
receives all granted as garden, gift.

Elegy for the Man in My Periphery

He's the one of tin roofs and swift storms,
the one who upended the night
to watch the moon drown.
He's the one who worshipped blight
and the battered dark, who savored
nightfalls that skinned trees alive
with that quick, failing light. Now
that he is gone, I may come to love
him, his name being my own,
even as I always missed him edge
the rain pits and marsh hummocks,
even as he shirked plain sight
to study the toothache tree's
leaflets, its blossoms' green-yellow glow.
One day I may come to understand
his refusal to love me back,
that lack like a nick
in the soft flesh between the thumb
and forefinger. And if there is one
thing I want to understand, it's why
he hitchhiked merely nine miles, hopped one train
and leaned into the fire of stars
to shroud himself in the smells
of sawmills and rusted coulters:
to murmur the name of someone he loved
just as they would walk away.
If he's really gone, why do the shallons
and shagbark hickories burn
with their understory?
Why do I see him now,
stalking apple and walnut groves,
where he stops to witness
the larvae of codling moths
writhe through every fruit?

The Child

Because there will be a child, grown from the pit
of the past, sky-whittled, seeded in the eastern pastures
>   of an Earth we will never know; because there will be
>   a child who walks a stream with feet evolved numb
>   such that blood leaks from her soles as she paces
the feldspar's sharp ridges; and because she will see
as many bones of humans as of bear and bobcat
>   and in her digging for worms witness

cellphones and scapulae, steel cups and prawns
of Styrofoam, she will not know what to make of this world.
>   Because there will be a child who is born
>   from something wombed by machine or flora or animal,
>   she will eat water hemlock just as soon as redhaw apples,
enough to keep her upright and unnamable (for she cannot name)—
>   and she will love the world such that all voids close behind her,
>   and she will know to tread carefully on September slopes,

when leaves fall and slip through mud to the creek
pocked with snakes—never cruel. And because the child will grow,
>   forged with eyes large as a pair of vipers' heads,
>   she will see the farthest galactic wedge with ease;
>   her mind will travel into its wieldy orbits and know all
stars that moor her to the Earth, and she will lie
down in soft grasses as days and wind and rains
>   pass over. All atoms will snarl their greenest mysteries

around her, and in her last dark she will know each of them
and their least trajectories, and no animal will blame
>   and eat her for their hunger, for the final heart's
>   renaissance will ripen green in her throat and burst
>   from her with a brightness borne of pure chlorophyll—
and she will grow and bleed for a million million summer-long days,
>   twine to the tips of squall-bowed trees. She will root herself
>   in the lowest creek and pulse in her new untamable nativity.

Upbringing

So sing hallelujah! as they douse the boy in river water.
So bring him up to find his eyelashes laced in silt—
so the congregants scowl at him, the odd one—
so red the mud smeared in his hair looks as blood gone slag with sin,
       he runs home in rain, his teeth chattering,

so the wind bites at him cold, even in May, the backroad mess
so bog-slocked and rock-slashed—and home now
so the family scatters from each other into their own nests,
so delicately built with least resentments—and the boy,
so tired, his ears crammed with biblical slosh, sleeps
so soundly, dreams of a girl he will never witness, her hair

struck red against the wetness of her white dress,
so lovely, lovely, that when he wakes he'll walk the farm
so pocked with nails and crates and lichen-licked pine and think never
so much as now of the clay that makes him, the water that shapes him
so heavily, this land a trap, a friend.

Summer, 1988

That year I rose most dawns
to birdsong, thrushes
and chickadees, the harsh
rasps of blue jays and melodious
bluebirds, then the clash
of pans thrown hard into cabinets,

my mother's crying, and more
than once glass shattering.
A child, every day seemed to me
a Sunday, for the creek's flow
seemed to enfold me into the beginning
of time again and again, and the overcast

skies tapped the least frightening shadow
and made the boulders that flanked
the water blunt as the hurt
that freighted my back—
universal as the atoms
that ate through my body.

One Sunday, my parents screaming
each other into another dusk's numbness,
I went farther up the stream's north oxbows
and found a small sparrow egg
cracked on a cleft of mica. The creature,
nearly hatched, stilled from a fall.

The embryo, almost bird-formed,
the head swollen big as a thumb
and the eyes no more than blue bruises
staring through itself into gray
grass battened to cold, lay wet
and newly dead. The trees

11

leaned in, somehow wrong,
somehow sinful as slatterns,
for I, a child, confused
by the grief I had carried with me,
thought the afternoon grayness
good as any rite or witness of sacrifice.

Why worship the guardians
that let one fall? In my mind now,
thirty years later, I can extend
my hand and touch the glistening
and fractured wing-form shot
through with red arterial streams.

I can hear the indifference of wind
at the shoals, the fragments of eggshell
and broken beak stippling the minerals.
This sight, clear as the thunder
of stars. This failed house now razed.

Persistent Trillium

Sometimes blooms are maps of stars,
and it will be a long while before we know it.
Sometimes this trillium is kicked to muck, but survives,
a small crowd of lanterns that rupture the dark

sealed breath of the Savannah River,
where no words rise from rhododendron slopes,
down gorges of the Tallulah and Tugaloo sluices.
And yet this trillium's tiny claim of land makes its own

language, delicate yet certain, the river
dousing it year after year through a humus
umbilical hymn to urge it to rise again,
to open its three glabrous eyes and steep in sun

well into July, when the sear burns
most other blooms alive. But now, under the stem,
the hem of this flower blooms dim
in the shade of the first day of spring—

the sun so slim the petals can't cling,
unlatch through the curl of this small valley
of wind, early dead and moonblown,
fewer and fewer seeding to genesis.

Anodyne

1.

Just north of Ward, South Carolina,
the pong of the paper mill writhes
the air southward,

across the orchards, all the way
to Johnston,
where creeks coil

through their motions;
small seeps carry through ditches
to and from my father's pond,

where catfish ripple
across the bottom, stir up
delicate skeletons

of their forebears. A stray dog,
wolflike, with a snout long and fierce,
with a lip-piece bitten and torn

from the bone so the teeth
forever snarl through that terrified life,
wails the tree line to savage prayer.

Up toward McCormick, a fire gnaws
through understory, destroys, renews.
The ash crosses

four counties.

2.

When I rise in the lonely hours
of the pre-dawn and a dark violet blossom
of fear turns in my stomach,

I hear my grandfather's voice.
I smell the cedar tang of his small house
in Troutman, North Carolina.

He told me once that, while fighting
in Iwo Jima, down deep in a trench canopied
in gunfire and the screams of the dying,

he saw a Japanese man's face
detach from the front of his skull
and fall like a huge, soggy leaf

down the hole to land on his shoulder,
the eyebrows and mouth still intact,
a grisly mask. Later, on Honshu,

a crazed boy
from Idaho threatened
to slit his throat

if he didn't let the him piss first in a bunker.
So my grandfather let him pass,
walked a few steps back,

and turned to see the boy explode
on a mine, a shard of metal
flying out of the jet of entrails

to lodge deep in his arm.
When I am angry, my envies
grinding down my heart,

I think of the sweat drenching
my grandfather's face, searing his eyes,
as he tried to rest

in the cover of scant trees
while shells boomed just a mile
downriver.

Then my anger shrinks in me,
and I notice how the wind sends
the high branches

to song. I notice how the trees scroll
through words of their own hidden language,
a lexicon behind perception,

a syntax of silences
that belie the violence
pulsing through our kind.

     3.

Down here in Johnston,
just east of the Savannah,
the iron-red snake that winds

between Georgia and Carolina, peaches
amplify under a sky thrummed with bees,
attune to field, bough, flower—

sometimes frost-silenced,
sometimes urged
to sweetness, the fruit

swollen wombs. Sometimes
the tongue cannot rejoice;
sometimes the psalms

of August shrivel
the heart to knot. So down
here, when summers growl

and scald creek-mouths
dry, hiss afternoons
with sudden storms, I watch

the woods and water for least gestures,
pray to know the singing
of the fox or kingfisher, elm or bream,

so that nights
when I can't sleep,
I can ride out

those creatures'
compound melodies,
their one and only hymn.

Sapphire

Once, in Franklin, North Carolina,
an old man with a snaggle-toothed smirk
and slyly kind heart planted one
in the bucket I hefted to the sluice
to dump and sift. Even in the shadow
of the long tin mining roof, the blue stone
that formed from the drifting sand stopped time:
Greek for "blue," when I peered at it, already
polished and cut well, I changed its angle
as the light gleamed through its dusk-sea shades.

That mountain town and all materials seemed
to assent to a small void in space where the storm-blue
stone had been (and was), in which a nebula
arced it parsecs-long body in miniature.
Or a prayer made mineral, ground to silence
and quantum-crushed into a blue particle of memory,
one I pocketed and still caress to harness
the dyed right hand of God.

Opossum

I've seen you die in ways I cannot measure—
the fall my dog snared you in her jaw,
bore you indoors, your retort
low, humanlike, a groan

foaming your crammed mouth.
She shook you so hard you came apart,
your guts sudden and delicate,
your life's fragments

so distinctly intact: your dark red liver
and gray intestines pasted to the wall,
and the heart, your heart I saw
throb out of you, still running

blood into your glazing sight. I did not sleep
for three nights, and finally, when exhaustion
warped me, you bumbled and careened
through my dreams,

stayed whole and faked a final stillness
that outpaced any cat, raccoon, or mutt—
You drooled in high branches,
your Boschian tail curled tight, bloody pink,

and of course, that hatchet-wound of teeth,
always grinning. I saw you shake off venoms
of rattlesnakes and cottonmouths
while you kept to peripheries—

but I knew the shape of your sagittal crest
and braincase, chilling as your vapidity,
alien as your courage and clamor
in the shed's darkest corners.

Yet now I long to hold you and stare
into your reckless eyes, grasp
the scope of my terror
as I endure you—

creature of the gray-and-dying,
spit-tooth, chasm-rat, strontium-bear:
I cast you from this nightmare rubble,
scream your praises to oblivion.

There Is Another Dwelling between Us

To the east of Troutman,
just past the broken brickyards
of Kannapolis, the rind of a town,

the thin yellow pall of chemical plants
gauzes the afternoon.
Chicken houses resemble the long, dark

outposts in dystopian nightmares
you keep having. In Burnsville, far north,
north enough to still clutch the chill

of this early spring, farmers find
solace in the disconsolate lovelessness
of their wives' mouths. The women

know the fields better
than the men—their inborn understories
outwit any gossip, weather, seed.

They know that rats and wasps
throb behind the drywall, that seasons
click arrhythmically

like a cleft metronome or heart.
At night they worry through their rooms
like nuns slipping into doubt.

The farmers, dead asleep, dream
of pumpjacks and silos in blood-red twilights
all spent, the land turning
its back for good.

Dissolved Gods

Over years, in some northern forests, where the firs
grow tall and stout, even as meltwater plashes
their roots, bears thrive beside rivers
and lash from swales and rushes

trout and salmon. When they have fed, their snouts
bloody in the dawn, they drop the fishes' skeletons
from which hang burrs of meat the bear's teeth could not wrest—
for decades these bones tilt and sink under glacial rains,

pulled under the tethers of sunlight and into dark.
And over years, when these delicate sculptures
collapse, the ground begins to sparkle
with specter-white fungi that drink the remnants

into slurry, crammed with minerals. Should the near
fir forest pay the fungi its due in sugars, the fungi
will exchange its strange unction with this underground milk,
and in the rings of trees the DNA of trout, salmon,
and bear will all urge the green needles farther into light.

Fall Again

into this favorite season, when the fields
     go stressed and gray, the attic groans
cold, and moths orbit the dusk before
     early dark. I want my life to be calm
as the apple blossom, the simple course

     of its unfolding, and the ease of being
like the flow of white petals on a creek
     after October rains, rarer now, or the moth
and its chalky transcription on the house's
     dark soffit, the lamps buzzed and shimmered

off. October tells me I cannot go back.
     I cannot revisit the flames of a boy's
tall hills when falls fell colder,
     when I watched the leaves unbolt
their inner lights and wind became a carnival of air,

     when time rang distant as cathedral bells.
October blocks paths back to morning's
     phantom spell, when my grandfather
had not yet faded like the dawn
     and dogs barked the days alive.

Where now is the guiltless spite I hauled
     in buckets choked with toads mined
from that gnarled oak just to tip them
     into creek-spray to watch them
tumble, wash away? I cannot struggle

     for life to play on the stream's high rims,
when one false step would have felled
     me, found me broken on the shale. October
does grant me one gift: a brew to mix
     these memories like music, a wind of bells

and apple blossoms, a sky of streams and moths
       and no ice yet—just the summer's blurred amulets
of stars now stark, clear as blight
       and memory that too will fail and fade
as any greenness from the voice.

Undermind

You know him: he comes during the cattle slaughter,
chaw juice matting his beard.

Always at auctions—buys snake skeletons, a book
of toxic plants, a book on witchery.

As if we could ever stop him, the one who cracks
every bone he finds to suck the marrow.

As if the grass weren't a kingdom, and his boot-falls
weren't a king's.

Smells of liverstink and frog legs. Smells of chicken
mills and a wall packed

with moldering rats. Shows up once a year at Yonce's
to stare at the woman

who sweeps their floors. Laughs when she flinches
at the spider sacs

built up in the corners. Makes the server
go back and forth for more lemon.

Mostly stares at the woman bent with broom.
As if he could dream

a nexus between them with his sniper eyes.
As if he could build then burn

with her in a house of blood, now partnered
in death to reveal each of his lethal cells.

Wild Pasture

Here the ghosts walk on past. At the last
turn in the paths small creatures have carved,
where locust thorns snatch our sleeves,
low-coiled briars burn in reddening light.
Something else stands between us

and where we are headed—
more than these nettles
in bent grass, more than the cold air
that strains the breastbone and teeth.

A few more steps and we might know
what lies behind the cracked door
on perception's edge, the light within
it the color of sweet backwater,
the kind that wants to be snowmelt,
so blue it hurts to witness, it hurts to taste.

So let's walk
through these slender asters,
bind the gap between silence and sibilance.

Let's watch the contexts of silences
as they turn like embryos in the many wombs
of air, wheeling in orchard sheds and the ossuaries
of distant pines.

Let's take these soft stones
and feel them to know their mother,
the glacier that birthed this pasture, nurturer
of knapweed and loosestrife, thorn moths
and cornflower
until the ghosts come back.

If we move on, they will lift their liquid heads
like strange birds and open
their throats, utter everything that is anther and tooth,
vein and door, answer what we have
yet to ask, their voices pulsing
through the bright seeds
of their mysterious hearts.

Self-Portrait as a Burning Cypress

So many ways to burn: when,
   for instance, the oil bleeds
     the swamp surface to formless

prisms, and a match flares the world
   red and shimmering, wild: when
     bowfin and minnows seek

the bottom's murk never to rise
   again, and the sin's catalyst,
     this kingdom of humid calm,

hoards the heat and chars my moss-
   wrapped limbs to roaring. Wood ducks
     scatter from the climbing blister

of my trunk to cane fields where
   crickets chirr early in noon-struck
     aster. But the story goes

back further, much further, back
   before any conflagration, any lantern
     or torch, any fireflies that sketched

the blunt edges of my body
   in their citrine light. Not even
     flasher moth or foxfire, ox-eye

or moonstone, and most certainly
   not the moon—for I can recite
     its names: dust, bone, shoulder.

It has no news. I choose to submit
   to the source, assent to the ruin
     of the sun itself, the light that blows

my leaves to cinder, forces
  me to my knees. To confess
    what my mouth, this earth, denies.

Grief Map

Dodd Hopkins lost his mind the day after his wife passed,
left his bed hours before the sun tipped the mountain's edge.
The morning wind was to his ear a prophetic tongue.

In sleeping clothes, barefoot, the moon's scant flame to light
his way, he walked into woods over briars and bramble
fully numb, wandered until dawn dipped the sky

in blue. He gathered all the flowers he could find, made
trips back and forth from woods to home with armfuls
of fringed phacelia, trillium, gentian, trailing arbutus.

The land's unsteady gable dizzied him, and, near noon,
his feet bleeding and the solar bath of light singeing his skin,
his brain absorbed the rate at which Earth spun.

He knew that no alchemies would summon
her, that no mix of ivy and thorn and blood would stall
the devils that carved the last of his sense away. He couldn't

shake the vision of her body underground, bleeding dry.
So he reaped and reaped until he felt satisfied he'd upset
spring's dark womb, made a hex of its design, and for weeks

more crept the ridges in mourning, snatching plants up
by fistfuls, his only solace the fibrous sounds of tearing taproot,
his smile the raveling of that embroidery.

He filled the house with her—blooms and leaves
took the shape her body had pressed into their bed. Nights
he cooked for two, placed wild onion and daffodils

in her supper chair. He lined apple leaves along the window
sills she used to crack to let the warmer seasons in.
Once he'd finished with the house, he transcribed her

into the winding path she'd tread in grass and mud
to tend their yard, to feed the garden until it fed them back.
And though all this work summoned her once or twice

to shimmer in his dreams, these steeped floras made the map
of grief he traveled every day, toiled to tend, even as all
he did to keep her there wilted, cracked, or blew away.

Prayer for Transposition

Let me, like flame, displace myself
into quivering arrays that caulk fallen limbs
in an ice-scorched field I have never seen.

Let me enter each blight of a brown eye's
iris, striking as unexpected snow, stunning
as dusk's first slur of starlight.

Let be my raveling mind, unbodying
each night to coiling flashing passage,
simple, severe as rivers after rain.

To a Minor Chinese Poet of the Kunlun Mountains

In your ancient and final hour,
when the moon scraped the horizon,
no longer a white fire
to guide you to the village of willows,

the ink had run dry,
your blood heavy, your spine
curved as the arc of distant lanterns.

When you sat, then collapsed into snow,
your strange verse fled
unperturbed down glacial streams
and into the starlit valley,

teeming with the glowing red fish
that drifted through your dreams.

So it is true no politicians ever championed
your scrolls that flashed
like dying stars
on which the eight immortals cast
their narrow immutable gaze.

So the villagers of Xianjiang
still swing their lanterns
against the dark woods, hungry.

From *Specter Mountain* (2018)

൰

Gatherers at Time's End

In the polar vortex, the tree limbs snapped loud
as gunshots, and I slept into a seeing of different
times, for time is an ovoid womb that gives

birth to dust, ice, and blood again and again,
that throws light back into itself until another time
is made. Numbed, I saw our cities

long darkened, not from cataclysm
or neglect, but from a human blossoming
toward the old utterance, the primal heart.

People scattered down the ridge
into the crimson stubble of valley to gather
around fires and sing the last words they could recall.

Snow piled on pines and blew off with rifts
of smoke. The wind still blew eastward, and the flare
of dawn still grayed into lilac into blue.

The fires forced the valley into an opening
bloom, and to hear the people singing was to know
them with love, to read them legible

as siblings. Such harmonies they made that my mouth
turned dry as years-old leaves. My body bent
into heavy narcosis. To know their rhythm

was to feel Earth gnaw at my own
measures, and to adore the world, hard as it is,
for finishing, always finishing, what it begins.

Chthonic

I sometimes fall into visions where the Earth
opens, and far underground, beneath the shallow dead
and the waterline, beneath any trace of life,

the world is undone, aortal and blistering,
glowing and darkening, the Hadean palpitant
center. Then, quickly, like human speech

played backwards to clipped silence,
the world sews its wound, and all the valleys
and rivers lean again into their time-worn complexities,

flourish and die, flourish and die. Sometimes it's best
to let the dream have its say and to snuff it to silence.
Sometimes it's best to outpace the tenacious ghost

of the unconscious, lest it follow you through days.
What then is a simple solace? The stand of light
between the trees? Perhaps I love the oaks

no matter where I am—on this mountain,
behind the cabin window, or near the stream
because I cannot endure the vision

of the buried body of my grandfather—a man
I could not love for his constant mantras
about the sinful and the end. His home was nearly pitch black

even on sunny days, any light a leaking toxin.
The only comfort he found was walking fields
in the pre-dawn half-light, always looking down, down

for arrowheads and bannerstones, quartz drills,
old pipes and bottles, some evidence that he moved
and lived, that others had gone, cast off their mundane

legacies. When I was seven, he reminded me I was
going to die. His visions chased and claimed him,
buried him early. Perhaps that's why the tallness

of oaks, their susurrus glittering
through the light, yokes me with astonishment,
a love I haven't learned to name.

I did not always live so high:
Once, miles down this ridge and into the piedmont,
I had a hound that dug deep into the loam,

crazed, wide-eyed. When he had bloodied his paws
and ripped roots asunder, he found what he'd been
after: a conch shell in perfect shape, a white spiral

with pink filigree. We were hundreds of miles
from any sea. The hound now lies in a midden
in those same woods, where for years red sumac thrived

out of him, his innards and ribcage,
the deepening caverns of his eyes.

Blackbirds

One late fall they descended into the valley
and amplified the bleeding trees,
cacophonies of the season's
undoing. We were afraid

that year: blackbirds often bannered
through the high air, their blurred
bodies a language kept hidden,
just beyond fluency.

Everything slackened, the kingdom
of weeds, even faith and old
tales seemed gimmickry,
the only tangibility

those blackbirds, their hive-minded
heaves from rhododendron
crowns. More than one
mind scrabbled

for some spark to snap the heart
to warmth, but nights
with the sharp stars,
those countless

distances, hazed into winter's
waking, when the morning
sun shredded to ribbons
of shadow

under the tenacious blackbirds—
and for a time the hinge
of Earth seemed locked
until those creatures

at last left us with a thin spring, long
after they'd cast dark
on our structured lores,
upset our old symmetries.

The Sisters

Brother, have you ever looked into the fire's radiance?
Have you witnessed the element up close?

What I've seen is buried deeper than the shards
that severed the floor with the flames' ranting shadows,

deeper than the first flush of the mountain's juvenescence
(for it was shallow and frost-killed), the only scents

those of ice and ash, no musky clover or apples—
deeper than summer roots or creek-wracked stones.

There in the night-delirious escape down the stairs,
hearing my father call for us, the roof roaring to splinters—

I saw the confused yawns of my dying sisters,
the flames so loud their yells fell through the beams,

blazing; their screams turned to rattle and rictus,
teeth and the spindle-wraiths, charred to spinsters

for the mud to take and worms to harness:
Tell me, brother, have you stood high in the mountains

and watched the stars spin over meadows, dead farms
where old airs sear and douse the tongue with silence?

Overburden

For now, the mountain is whole. For now,
the galax and foamflower thrive beyond
themselves. And when wind whorls in
the topmost branches of hickory,

ghosted notes strum in a minor key.
For now, the valley meadows resume
their florid sparseness, void
of any aspect of the old mountaineers

who were the last to leave, save the pine
and cedar planks of their cabins now long
collapsed, the mosses gnawing away those
sigodlin geometries. And in the many

doorways that open into the mountain
where liminal craters of breath can still
be felt, just barely, one might smell pangs
of rust, salve, medicine, or soap, soon

overwhelmed by the mineral tang of stone.
On these sheer edges
where the earth heaps or strips away,
the spring is still a seamstress, the summer

a kiln. These hills burn within
the cosmos, the flesh contained in land
filled with dimming lamps of stars. For now,
the valley's creel washes up in aster.

Wild dogs creep beneath shards
of dusk the limbs reshape.
Mountain lions satisfy their bloody motions.
For now, the mountain is whole.

Questions for the Mountain

Why do you remain still in the human season?
Because your season is fleeting, and you are as broken as I.

What do you feel when your garments glow in fall?
The fire scalds me just as it would scald you.

What do you think of those who have hewn your sides and build?
What they build molders in one quadrillionth of a nanosecond of earth-time.

Do you not feel pain from how men have craved and carved you?
I have felt a pain beyond your reckoning.

What will I see in your creeks in the warmer seasons?
You will see what I allow you to see.

What may I witness?
Trout-curve and moss, one reading of water, one reading of stone.

What will you keep hidden?
All readings of worm, carcass, tree flux. Any true reading of water.

Why would you hide anything from me?
Because you are a mite that forms one particle of all refraction.

Why do the wild plum trees bend so low in your shadows?
Because no sun tilts there any season save the first week of spring.

How can I bear part of you away with me?
You cannot. Any stone cleaved from me is no longer my body.

Where can I hide from the fear that gnaws within me?
There are many deep swales here. There are many yawning gorges.

Have many hidden here?
Many have hidden here.

Are you then a gravestone reared up by those many sorrows?
I am a cradle, an engine, a cenotaph.

Does time move through you with greater clarity?
I suffer time a million million times over.

Are there phantoms here?
Yes, and you are one of them.

Even as I live and witness you rise with your brothers?
I speak of the man-that-is-you who moves before you move.

Are there any phantoms behind me?
More than all the stars your eyes were made to see.

Why can't I see them?
Because you are a mite that forms one particle of all refraction.

Have I hope of catching the phantom that moves before me?
*Even if you do, another phantom will outpace him, then another, then
another.*

Forever?
Forever and ever.

Father

Dear father-of-this-mountain, my father,
I have no story to tell. I have few words
to say while the ants infest and bear
away the lynx's carcass and maggots

sprout to eat away every last morsel of self.
When my ear hits the pillow, I hear only
my pulse—it betrays everything, offers
no wise gossip. It thrives alone.

Nights I dream you under an overcast sky,
somewhere on the southeast slope,
tucked in a pocket of hemlock
where the streams converge

into quick rushes before long winter rains
slow downstream, the water clear,
bearing up to sight every stone.
Father, I dream of underwater

rivers, my vision wavering, the moon
big as a chine. I dream within this dream,
become a rainbow trout dashing
into water grasses, then a bear prowling

through diamond hedges of new snow.
And when I become the creature
with eyes that can decode your form,
you shatter and fall like winter.

Father-of-nothing, I am the product
of Bible and babble, of glossolalia
thrown against moon and mountain—
both throwing any utterance back,

for they too are echoes. Father,
there's thunder coming over the lower pasture—
there's fire coming over the ridge,
hymns of ablution, of effacement.

Father, I love you. You are not a wilderness.
You are not the fox that lopes away. The valley is
not a cradle. The valley is silence so complete
it blares through the hills a woeful howl.

Brother

Brother, who knits the winters
with dour albs of rain?

Who taps the stamen and milksap,
untethers the sleeping seed?

Brother of barns and lordly muscles
of horse pasture, it is time

to say goodbye—the white trees
rise to bluest morning, the austral slowness

of spring. This is a darkening,
too: the silver peach blossoms

laden by gravity and pesticides,
histories, stone and rust, bone and blood

and well before when these hills formed and stretched
higher than the Alps. The millennia rolled on

and shaped the rock that we now reshape.
We choke all-time

for our single hour. The land
has not yet said all it must say—

one syllable of its utterance
is slower than one thousand summers.

Brother, we get older; time quickens,
disperses, starlings at the field's edge.

Memory becomes seasonless,
strange, and the bloodroot

curdles to foam near the river.
Brother, before we part,

let's walk one last time
down to watch the creek,

where vestige apples
melt to sugared slurry,

stunted by the mass
of their own beginning.

From *Creeks of the Upper South* (2016)

&

The Single Star: Prophecy and the Unforeseeable

1.

We walked into the valley of dark, our sight

        pinned to the ember of the single star the falcate moon
could not douse. We learned the blue bowl of air

        had tipped and littered the valley with grass, delicate as hair
and changeable as water for the shuttered eye (changeable as stone,

rhythmic as blood-crux in salamander or goat,
rhythmic as the green core of moss or elm).

       ℘

For years my mother smelled of sour bread.
I'd carry her down the mountain in the blue dark
on my back near the swale where we'd build a fire
in the summer cold.

The bones behind her face had sunken, and I saw her pulse
tick shallow in the shadow of her throat.

Her voice was no more
than leaf crackle,
no more than kindling.

2.

What She Remembers:

That in the summer of her seventh year,
storms slanted in and engorged the rivers
and creeks until all waters buckled high,

shattered the levies and bit to the quicks of berms:
houses that did not kneel and drift away moldered.
They moved the whole town eight miles north.

That in her ninth year she came back to the creek
then in drought and walked barefoot
the dry bed's limb-trash and alabaster—

That something in the slim sun-spears made
her look up into the unshackling of April
and witness a horse skeleton. Brown-white

as the soles of her feet and silty hands.
She looked long at how vines twined in brisket,
at the strange philodendron head, drained

of flesh, brainless and almost comical in
its stillness, staid and smiling long with gothic
joy at the sheer oddness of how the Earth had reined it.

That the winter of her thirteenth year
in the frigid mineral scent of dusk, the Harman
boy breathed warmth on the small hairs of her neck,

the whiskey on his child's breath, how they leaned
into one another on the blindness and purity
of the killed grass beside the creek, the water frozen

pure to the floor, where stunned curves
of minnows flashed tinny and motionless
under the stars' arc-light.

That the thaw snapped and pocked the air like gunshots
so that in the first hint of spring the Harman brother
slew the boy she kissed and dragged his kin down into the gorge.

3.

What She Cannot Foresee:

That centuries the white window of the moon will open,
house roofs will crumble as the horse bones gripped
in the long-fallen oak will fall themselves, then grind

down with years, fold with dust and meld with the specks
kept there of the murdered boy, millennia-old, both
now in the earth proper, slack and laggard slow.

Sanguinaria

In the chill before Easter, it was dusk again,
and my mother and I walked the berm, out past

the corn. The night's door warped: the sky
broken from its hinge swung down

low to us, low enough that the smell of rain
steeped our hair. Behind the springhouse,

we stopped to watch a possum crawl
over a years-old midden

with such reckless fear she took a spade to its skull.
How can I justify a fear that blooms in the gut

and stings like thistle? Such creatures follow
me in my sleep, the ones harmless but foul,

the ones that must haunt: blowfly, centipede,
wolf spider, the bubbling muck of toads.

We trudged into watercress, across the field,
she in her country gown, a ghost before me—

down to the hemlocks and galax
when the rain fell sudden, and the wind

pierced the thicket and drowned our scalps.
There is no such thing as empathy.

လ

The storm drove through, just north
of us, a great spectral womb broken, ripped.

Our footfalls hugged the creek side's silence,
its washed-out whisper. Its sealed mouth.

There with her in that violet cold. All the blood
that ran through that shadow. All the bloodroot

we smashed through. The bloodwort,
puccoon root slanted into fields two

farms over, up from the rushing creek curve
where heaped stones were draped with lichen.

The moon smeared behind clouds, a runnel
of milk. Why does the sight

of lanterns dawdling in a far pasture
ignite the heart with joy and sorrow that, upon sleep,

the mind lumbers with false memories of farmhouses,
days and days of threshing grass, the chirp

and grind of crickets in the core of a summer long dead?
The rain fell hard: we quickened through briars, up

to the back door, the red light that framed it.
She said nothing. I witnessed her face

turning in the window—a shivering
leaf that withered, that would not release.

Bees

When I was six, my mouth smeared
        with sugar, I stumbled into my uncle's barn
where I heard them thrum inside their hex maps

behind the slats, a sentient wall I could hear tremble—
        They glowed grainy in the sun-slants,
the afternoon deepening to evening, seemed drunk

on June heat and that chapel-light, that hot, slow stifle.
        I got too close, and the few outside that bobbed
around the high ricks zigged and zagged,

one mad enough to dart into my hair and send me
        scrambling. It stung. My face throbbed,
the blood grinding, sloshed with pain,

my sight fuming with a fuzzy nimbus that framed
        my dash back to the house where my uncle
plucked the stinger and rubbed a tobacco clump

dipped on calamine into my scalp. They haunted
        my sister, too, stung her nearly every summer,
and for revenge we'd smack them with swatters,

heap their bodies in a blue Mason jar we kept
        on the kitchen's windowsill
until we'd killed so many they began

to spill over the rim, fleck the floor. We swept
        them up, capped the jar, and walked
them down to the creek where we poured them

into the flow, their bodies flashing over sandstone,
        alabaster, some stopped by limbs,
most swirling like tiny lanterns down the water

and out of sight. Now, right now,
       a honeybee drones around the door frame,
and I like the heft of its flight,

the click of its spiracle against the wood.
       I open the door to let it loose into this April
made sweet by its kind, its world's flawless

vectors. It flirts with a pink trumpet flower,
       its coarse song tingles through my scalp,
greening memory, spring wind.

Self-Portrait as Epiphyte

I dream
myself on salt trees and salverform
near rock rose, all plaited

till I wake. What is this but prayer?
Look: the starlight sways
the pond to utterance,

and down in peat worms harvest,
scald through flesh and root, while above,
shoots shake the day to pulse—the floating

heart greens water, bream stone-vital, burly
weave through the sun's scattering light—
I steady my brain to larger form,

graft my body to trunk
and another, log mass and calyx,
premonition of every seed, every star.

Six Vespers

After a long time when the fall tells its lie
the water lowers the hills are steep with shadow
and the feet find uneven ground, rooted clots,
sharp passage, and a man is nothing but bone under
the shale the rotten wood gone, his skull,
smooth after centuries, the rictus of his smile beautiful,
the redness his blood now washed by forces
of dawns springs of ice-melts summer-held and flared
undulate and myriad, disorganized as memory,
the arteries gone to the subatomic outwash
of a fallen body: Father of a broken time,
mother of frostweed whose child has risen into a terrible season,
into winter's transfixed hands, gnarled by clouds:
bluest storms gray fingers striking the elms like matches:
Tell me where to turn. Northeast breach and frigid stars
tell me how to drench—How does your arc singe
numb the heart, brand the body,
stoke the brain to blast the pulse
from ember back to palpitant growth warmth
to flame to grain and scar? sewn?

Three Notes on Drowning

Once I drowned
in a pond
life-dark
as a window
shuttered and damned
by moss and mildew—
My breath left
me in a basket of streams,
took me to the source
of the stitch, and under
water, I saw all the many
faces of God in the egg-
clogged country of fish
dens and water grasses,
the November-silver
darkness of trees decades
submerged, their surfaces
glowing with the pox
of iron and bilious
leaf flagellates, bruised
and undulant, aqueous,
mildly threatening
then benefic
as the sun broke
on the tree line

I drowned
in a gar-gouged current,
sun-spiders crawling,
made of eyes
blinded
mended by the mouth of water—
lung-crammed, crushed
woven, the drag
glutting my brain
the flux of perception, the blue
creatures, diatoms, paramecia,
forced through this skeleton-
turtle, snake, gar
wavering with the thermal,
shimmering and sentient
old, fiery,
not without poison,
the toxin-drainage
trash
bloomed sudsy
though fresh life
emerged, adaptive
as all creeks are good
like yolklight fire
the oldest smoldering

The Blue Child

Dusk gone dark now and the boy not home, they walked
  the oak ridge to the quarry to find the body
    branch-caught in shallows. Honeysuckle, fireflies.

Approached his small form stretched on the water face-down
  and bobbing gently. Turned him over to find the boy's lips black,
    throat shrunken and withered in its struggle to inhale air

where there had been none, his chest caved smokeblue. Top left of his
  forehead cracked—a red lightning stitched from skin to skull.
    Somehow he'd swung on the rope wrong, let go and tumbled

to the sharp edge where the stone gouged him nameless. How
  many hours like this, now almost dark and with the night a coming storm?
    There was a wind and the man looked back at his wife to find her

hair masking her features sideways. Her mouth burled, her hands
  in mid-gesture. Sounds of the earth
    ceased, the clouds moving spectral over her. Starless. Blanked.

꙰

She went to rise to the false heaven of her upstairs bedroom,
  and he drove through the months eye-locked on distances he could
    not claim. The boy's things burned, cast off. His father's mantra,

unspoken, latched:

I have trees grown nodal with hives.
That bees should rouse and drag me
down through sorrow.

I have creeks where sculpin and spiders
blend with stone. That I should go
there and swallow water hemlock

*to seize my heart, shut my throat
and drain all dry.*

Understory

And now we will witness the unseen flames:
cardinal shit, apple maggots, fishbone thistle, squama
and fauna scales, keratinous flakes flecking ground;
sporiferous trees (ambassadorial as they kneel);
hyssop, sometimes odoriferous; dried blood on bark,
dropwort, smartweed and sweetleaf; outhouses
still standing in a crush of woods (redolent of peaches);
early-century crates breaking under the weight of wild squash;

crimson minnows courting a swale (painterly over chalk-white silt
and rocks stroked with moss so green it hurts to look);
woad and its micro-cache of bluest rivers; witloof chicory
(good in salads); distant farmhouse windows on winter nights
shining like citrine stricken with sun; the yucca's
blades curdled with cream-flowers a few April days;
jars of milk; smell of leaf-fire; poxy bogs

emeralded with mosquito eggs; itchweed, abelia,
and spittlebugs with their soapy secretions;
the half-buried bones of cats, their skulls
ghastly and beautiful; musket balls buried (for good);
possum oak and possums themselves (drooling
and conspiratorial in suburban sheds);
ivory nuts and ivy-tods; the helix-lattices of lichen;
gypsum and hagberry; the toothless kin-gone elderly

who grin at the edges of cracked doors (kind or wary);
snakeskins, fraxinella (burning bush); understory
flames; diatomaceous earth; the waxy cartilaginous
bulbs of rocky shoal spider lilies; cutworms that gnaw
on vegetable seedlings so that they fall like small timbers;
capillary mattings (wicking water from reservoirs);
wild decay (never gothic) and wildest (never lofty) revival.

Elegy Where the Creek Quits Discussing Itself

Now there will be times when your words
disappear, taken into currents and sealed,
not only when winter shuts the water's mouth
and frost builds its trellis glow across
the banks of starlings and all the way up
through the hemlock and rhododendron
to blend with the moon's axled light, but too in summer
when your body ebbs, nyctitropic as any bloom
that raises its head against the dusk—

and still the eye rooted in your sleeping brain
will dream the town falling, the cars
all slowed to a stop, the piles of tires
plundered by the woman with the scarred face
who took the fire of a burning house
completely into herself, whose face
changed so much it reminds others
that they are no bridge into each other—

this woman just wants a chance
to feed herself—and in the dark
where it never occurs to anyone to think
of her, she leans into her deprivation,
stalks the woods for berries, minnows, grass,
anything—for her, it might as well be winter
always, every grass blade a fleck of frost-light—
and little more for her than the dawn's long
red cirrus, the unreachable geese

that blast the morning air and vanish
into the inconstancy of clouds. Then you will leave
the thought of her, too, as wind flutters
over this erodible ridge. When the pines
tremble, you will notice, just for a moment,
the beast that shrouds itself in ciphers:

scarlet sage and harbinger-of-spring,
slushy driveways and red gas cans, the tall, lying
queen of this land, her galling silence.

From *Tree Heresies* (2015)

ଞ

Prologue

1.

You have taken a road into a place you do not know—
off the green cusp of mountains, or up from sand-stung
marshes, you are here and you are

here: Down piedmont dusks where soils
meld from loam to clay to dust and back to loam,
a wavering pedosphere, home to plum and scuppernong

over which bats fling themselves blind, demon-toothed
through barn lofts and lamplight, over silos and water towers
and miles-off county roads where stars now rise.

Where sparrows make houses of ruined chimneys
and storms roar from nimbus gourds
poured by phantom giants to set peach trees steaming,

caught between here and the other world. Where foxes
scream the woods to sacredness,
and owls crouch the limbs phantom-eyed to watch

for mouse-skitter or skink. In creeks red minnows gather
in still pools, each eye fastened to a wavering instant.
Water moccasins drag the black fires of their bodies

into limestone fractures, their torsional smolder
unseen. Wind bends east through thicker flora,
and gangs of mange-pocked dogs lope and skulk

in their lusts and through low woods fireflies constellate
sumac and bamboo. Below, milk caps and devil's
urn sprout alien, clustered. Leaves open: east-most fields fallow

with neglect. A swamp stagnates, impaled with a derelict
truck, mattresses, a charred tractor and heaps of cattle bones.
Hundreds of glass bottles, jars. Moldering possums. Trash-richness

growing shoreward, piling up grass banks gone toxic,
only to collapse again into this smutty stew.
Surface's oil haze, prismatic. No life in this water.

Near these earthen cancers a high shed with music, coarse
laughter where farmhands gather to myth out their emptiness
in tequila and cervezas, lewd jokes. Faces soot-smeared,

sunbrowned, smiling raucous, muscled. Eyes half-mast
and brains staved pattern and drone. For what can the heart
carry from this place? And what is home but the distant

windowdark where thin flowers sprout from the single
sill's empty can? Crucifix pollinated in nicotine.
Yards where grass will not grow, where women break

yearly and yearly until nights drain dreamless
toward their husbands' pre-dawn orders. Trucks huff
morning's swelter. To rehearse the orchard

into mass, leave it bone.

2.

Townward, field's edges matted in leaf-litter decades old, clogged
in the pox of sweet gum saplings and glass.
An earth igneous, ignored.

This land flat save the sheer knolls of creeks
flushed with summer storm, heliophilic
silences that drain into copse creeks.

Pervading smells of sawdust, iron, gasoline. Maws of
private wells, groundwater moon-doused. Fields
shunted upwind with train howls, window rattlers

forcing in slumbering country brains dreams
of churches burning, the ax chopped wrong to hack
blood from body, hex and freak of late April frost.

Ghost-choked country. Where no ear
stops for story lest metaphor siphon Bible tongue,
lest image shake loose weathers to kill the seed.

3.

One church in town, caustic architecture, white
and sheer, the steeple rusting starward. Orthogonal
spectral force to town streets and dark therein.

Shops of snuff, tobacco, little candy tins, pipes,
knives and nails, the smells of metal, oil,
and sweetness so rich they dizzy passersby.

Now the clerks exit their backdoors, tired,
retreat from wares into brick alleyways,
into structured dark, somewhere they call home.

County's south where new roads untether the horse
forever, the asphalt's bitumen, exhaust and rubber smells
confluenced with rotten peaches, skunk,

the flower stench of walnuts, carried clear and pure
to the county's north tip. Here, a phalanx of older trees,
tall and conspiratorial, panoptic, swaying.

A backroad twines to a gravel driveway flanked in poplars, coils
serpentine for a quarter mile up to a brown Victorian house,
large porch with swing and hydrangea hugging

the perimeter. Inside, immaculate sadness:
china behind glass, a polished dining room
table set for two but never used, all beds bed-skirted

and the attic spiderless. Cellar jar-clogged
with jellies and beans to keep years. So clean
a patch of dust strikes the eye sexual.

Kitchen floor lit in squares of failing light, and on
the counter a saucer of butter softening. No one
here, no sound save the ticking of joists and ceiling

corners. Old sepia pictures of frowning forebears
mid-field, or family portraits, hardships rendered
in furrowed brows, hard-bled flesh and land.

4.

Upstairs, she turns in her pain. Smells
of soap and tea, smells of her hair strung
white with sweat, harrowed sleep.

Bedsprings groan. Her long breath. Wordless
and still, supine, eyes cordoned off from joy.
The house cold with dark, even as behind it

now the falling sun gloams blood-red over
this patch of orchard saved for blood kin—
these fragile trees sugaring night-wind.

5.

Here he walks, slow, lumbering, drunk
on day's vestige heat, cloud's downslant
through tree line, the distances of far-off towns.

To stand this ground now and tame
days to peaches, profit, to lift, till and spray,
to help his hands cull back the days.

To stay here till deepest twilight, boots still on loam,
leaning faint and moonburnt into what he cannot change.
Glances back houseward to the high window,

lamp snuffed, knows she stares dead-eyed at nothing,
a nun to her lost son, to the snapped umbilical
years where memory is water and his end.

From that day on, the moon to her: a roving eye.
From that day on, any gladness in him
algebraic or underling to the unmovable:

the near woods' creek flow and oxbow silicates,
deep arrowpoints long buried, lodged for millennia:
clovis, bannerstone, half-dimes and knapped chert.

Hidden narratives of creek-side mothers, onyx-haired,
laughter and bowls boiling with hunted meat.
Clothed in deerskin, turtle shell rattles for the green

corn dance. Villages gathered at rivers to fish
and feed over fires beneath vegetal gods.
Now only stone: Quartz, schist, silt.

English pipes. Beads and awls, novaculite drills,
pottery shards, flint scrawls and scraps stitched
through remnants of animal and human alike,

stone-ghosted testimony in underground layers no human
shall see again. Still downward, Pleistocene imprints,
amuleted dents of moon-old gestures, cruxed

in bivalves and bryozoans, earth of Pangaea
before stromatolites and Hadean protohistory, magma fire
and comet, dust and this turning galactic allusion.

Aubade for Yellow Jacket

Dawn light sets them smoldering,
tiny gold-black fires that scorch the yard's
heart. They pulse: in, out, in, out

of a mud-ringed tear, where their crazed
focus seeks wood-pulp for nested tiers.
Guards click, seethe for queen and brood.

Something hums under this hill,
an open mouth that sucks the searing
sugars every June drips. Something

chews earth to paper dust and builds
these buried cells well into day's end,
when most dusks fail to douse

summer-stubborn heat. Grass crackles:
such a drone, a throb of anger here.
Hard to hate them for this madness

to outdo what will do them in, as fall
bleeds queens to flakes and new kin
hatch, winter-hidden, waiting.

Nocturne for Cicada

Down where the pines scuff the moon,
they rattle the woods to whir and static,
scrims of sound, vatic music so loud

at times it lodges in the ear like a burr,
carries through sleep a soundtrack
of farmhouses under stars, the slant

land's windfall leaves they settle in to scar.
Red-eyed dusk-chisels: they whittle the mind
so sharp it conjures collapsing ice

on a pond at winter's bladed end,
a crack in the attic window. Fork tines
clicking on a clean plate. The miracle of a silver

pocket watch unclasped and ticking still
after years locked in an oak-white box. To scrape
and sing the sun down, swell cedar

and elm through wind and wind time
back to earth's first songs. To play
that instrument, counterpoint the night.

Barn Gothic

Red as a cardinal, it leans ruined in winter's gray field,
form falling against a sycamore,
                  its older, wiser wife.

Closer in, a fox den
in the hay tunnel light where green eyes haunt
           the nearby mountain woods and stars cast

silver glyphs on the rotting floor:
Rain has felled the structure's roof.
            Here horses pitched and leaned

into chaff, awaiting work,
this room still alive in smells of oil, dung,
           and cedar-heart. Swallows twig

warped boards, black widows
      float, wait
           in corners to wrap and gore what passes.

Wasps caulk the loft's cracked seams,
and mice hide from owls, eyes,
         their lives the barn's heart

beating behind the walls.

Horsemint scent finds
the barn's chinks. Moonflower
        grips, twines

the rusted scythe and the burled
yawn of the caved-in door: Earth
        sculpts without consent,

remnants hallowed, restored—
Autumns, when the air shucks
               summer rain to hollow starriness,

the moon strikes the barn just right:
White moths hoard here where lanterns
               have long been snuffed,

where the only fires are the moths themselves,
their flock come to love this place and perhaps
               the stars, too, all pure, radiant, dying.

Nightmare, Revised

Now it is not a man pinned eviscerated
to a barn door and stretched mothlike
to show his brisket,

the drying jewels of his innards
and his teeth red-tinged, eyes
scappled bald. Now it is

not a plum-colored sky over
foothills of ruined chimneys,
the world forever November.

Instead, I stand in a field where there is
no barn, and the pinned man, my father,
has been let down, sewn back to life:

He walks through his home, his loneliness
a dark carapace. His mother lies
in a pine box in a South Carolina

graveyard. By now her eyes are fused
and sunken. By now her mouth is
a leather smudge. She wanted cremation

but the family would not have it.
The bones of her fingers poke through skin—
The moon impales the night.

The smell of smoke blooms on the sweet-sharp air,
and I feel a joy under the thin arbor
of passing clouds.

I feel a joy, because there is no secret order
of moth or plum, chimney
or chelicerae, only the pungent fact

that somewhere, somewhere beyond my sight,
a fire burns part of this
land gone, gone.

Boyhood Trapped behind the Eyelids

We knew nothing that summer
      summoned the grasses and stars,
            were maps for our skin as we ran

through leaf-litter, the sweet juice
      of scuppernongs sugaring our throats
            and fat hornets in their paper

nests hanging like scorched cauls
      and through the night-woods where
            we broke into the skitter of goat bones—

The ancient man from Africa whose visage
      pruned through the windy leaves
            in the dull lamplight—and how we dreamed

of the olive complexion of the older girl's
      breasts she'd let us see one day in the
            loft, and even a flash of the peach-fuzz

cleft behind her panties so that nights
      I ached and tried to will her candor
            beside me, over me, under me, her

breath hot in my eyes and her cheeks
      flecked in olive freckles. And into fall
            when the ridge of peach trees swelled

into a galaxy of red-pink planets, we took
      to orchards and made forts to hide
            and witness with a child's fear

migrants weave and yell in truck beds
      treading the clay rows. And October's swollen
            twilights folded us into the unspoken

knowledge that our blood was our fathers'—
      our blood pulsed our shapes
            into the sculpture of our kin, when

winter took over and the snowdrifts skinned
      the sky of its blue muscle to render
            the whiteness of full cold,

forced us into the heat of ovens and mothers to watch
      the blur of each other in the gauzed glass of windows next
            door, to wait again for springmelt's warm throb.

Lantern Sparrow

When the shadow of sleet fell across the bed,
I entered a sadness I had never felt before,
where sparrows flew through snowfall to find

the white scrabble of my yard and the house's
charred remains still smoldered. A lone flue
stood gnarled, half-collapsed. One sparrow landed

there on the blackened brick, preened as snow
fell runic and skewed in the dusk while the quarrel
of its kind, the hundreds it had come with,

bannered away through cedardark, the frigid,
moonless air. Its gray-brown dullness seemed
to bend the winter stars down

the gray-brown distance—until at once
its heart and tiny bones glowed from within.
The garnet lungs and ruby heart. Lantern-sparrow,

ghost-sparrow, sparrow of country roads gone
to the snowlight of spilled milk. Bird-of-ember,
bird-of-ruin that made me love the beauty,

the austere purity of that nothingness. Had I
that sparrow, I would call it kin, have it sleep
in a tiny basket of grass at my feet, let it haunt

the attic's beams and rafters. If the sparrow
were mine, I would ask it nothing about the night,
only savor its palpitant clarity, its warmth in my hands.

Shawnee Trail

Near the creepweed, a roadkill hare, the head
fully detached from the rotten torso,
the ribs shattered, browned in sun.

No vulture, no alms. The trees, still
as graves, dark smudges on the gauze
of afternoon. The sun, a blinded eye.

Soon, the moth-light of evening, when gullies
shine, ditches of pentecost until full dark,
when a single firefly coils like a ghost seed

down the dusk's throat. Moments lost
in death and beauty, death and beauty.
Fine: Let summer break its back again

on hidden stones, the wilted leaves,
the trillion vines that search the dark
for something to clutch and conquer.

Attic and Image

When the attic door collapsed from the ceiling,
we looked up into that rectangular dark and smelled
the must of years weep down into the lit spaces

where we walk and speak and sleep and eat. Dusts
of moldering apples and a blue-stained wedding veil,
a crush of naiads that hatched and cored

from a wayward cowbird who happened, one
frigid December, into a darkness not its own.
And in all that still haunts us from this dull heaven,

the day's vestige heat, the musk of storm-fraught
rafters that bend and warp in perfect anonymity,
the bony profile of that bird, kept in the dark bird-shaped stamp

of dust on the curved sill of the attic window
that I have not seen but know is there,
that bird-shape blasted by the sun and haunted

by stars for decades in this normal house on a normal street
with its normal consent to gravity,
that image is what I take with me now to sleep.

Tincture

First wood smoke scent on the wind—
      lungs twinned full of fire's sharpness,
charwood ghosting down through a northeast
      growing colder. Land of chimneys

and Bibles. When all creatures begin
      their hidden dens, when mornings spin clearer
and the moon slices through day's blue doxology—
      One star dies there, remnant mineral

that shimmers and unshackles fall's fluency,
      unwinds the body into trestle and scar.
Not honesty, but clarity that mothers the eyes
      into the dimming, imperishable pasture.

Furnace and Fox

1.

Tonight so clear the Milky Way shimmers like a stoked furnace,
the scattered stars like rogue embers deep in a bloomery.

I recall my father's face, the orange light of the wood stove
imprisoned in his skin, his eyes trapping the firelight

until he'd lobbed and poked the pine logs, then shut
and latched the grate. The chimney roiled the wind

with the sweet-sharp scent of charred trees, a smell
that I catch tonight through the open window despite

the lingering scent of a cold rain that's come and gone,
rushed and vanished over town like smoke.

2.

That was the year my father smelled of tobacco and rum,
leather and stone, the year the house creaked hollow,

ticking down into the gravity of his loneliness. That was the year
his silence began in earnest, the months he embraced

his bitterness, mantled it on his body like a second skin.
Nothing mattered then save the language of the woods—

the single plum tree sprouting tiny, sour hearts, the bullfrogs'
blaring counterpoint to owls that never asked any question,

only swooped to snag a shrew or mouse and disappear
back into the darkness of their hunger. That winter, the nights

were stitched with screams, half-human, half-angel, Nephilim
wails that braided through trees so loud they woke one

from deepest dreams of attics afire, of possession lost to the throat
of flame. They woke one to stand dizzy and stumble numb-footed

out into the cold with no malice, only dazed wonder at the face
that glowed low from the dead leaves: a fox so still and obsessed

it became a creature of ruby, of snow-mask and bloodroot—
a creature whose radiance granted my father rare joy, first healing.

In Fear of Silence

Tonight, in pain, I lean into the blueness
of dusk after reading poems to a crowd:
No one follows me into the ground-
lit corridors of western

South Carolina, where pines jag the moon's
belly, and orchards kneel under stars.
No one can hope to understand
these fields' rapt emptiness.

Once, I saw a man walk far-off in the faint
glow of a streetlamp just off the northtip
of Yonce's packing shed. He had clearly
lost his mind. Even at that

distance, I could hear him barking at twilight,
screaming *You goddamned better give me
back my mouth.* He vanished in high
weeds and I heard what Christ

allows: the truck engines of teenagers murderous
with boredom, bullfrogs, the human screams
of rabbits dying in their dens. The houses
ticking gaunt and lean, long and crumbling

in the fullness of every season—silence here
the one necessity, the one stone that freights
every tongue lest someone dare suggest silence
and silence only beyond the sun.

Hour

If I walk the sun-killed grass
among the farmlight of summer
mornings where I know

my footsteps alter forever
the shape, the calculus
of this earth;

if I step through gray stones
of old rail yards at night
when one blue star

claims the seam winter pines allow;
if I move through evening's
blood-stained hours

and the briars scrape, drag some
of me with them into roots;
if I consider old men

gum their memories on skewed
porches across these fields—
the dimmed weathers

of their minds grown colder,
the woodpiles of their years
now cindered cauls—

and if I admit the world is
kind, even as it murders
my cells and days,

even as it kills, sculpts my joys
into a hidden box of bone,
dust, and worm,

my heart blooms orchard deep
to know this earth has made for me
an hour of seasons, seeds,

and sentience, for which I am
nun, priest, imam: married
to all it withholds.

Flowers in a Northern Field

The heart draws to what it does
not know: Not arctic, but north
enough for purple saxifrage
to grow: Perhaps near Halifax
in autumn, when trillium or trout
lilies wilt in upper meadows,
and rime climbs the loosestrife
spikes until they bow and crack:
north, a mythic north, where
baneberry and blue-eyed grass
flux gorges through a colder
country, where crux and mind
can witness, gather, come home
to warm beside the glowing pine.

Spring Walk, Dusk

Out past the suburbs,
into kept land where
distance still sings hymns
called *clarity*, mind finds
itself bowered, grown to
language beyond tongue—
Cornflower sky and this
road's curve where wisteria
weighs down itself, spilled
to ground like blue-young
nebulae. Memory's blue
brain made solemn in galaxies
of pollen, sexed earth
sprung in moth-hordes,
moss. Stars strewn above
this spinning dark, all
leaves shrines of bluest
fire, vestige light.

The Milk Witch

Her head wrapped in torn red rags,
her fist clinched red around bail,
she edged down to the broken
waters of Moon Creek at dusk,
her tongue dry as winter stone,
sludged through the ice-shelved oxbows,

and came upon gooseberry
bushes not yet bloomed. She cast
a towel of soft silk twill
on their bare twigs and limbs, wrapped
them hidden like some mountain
Arachne, let the ends hang

down to brush the frigid muck.
Next she tucked the iron pail
beneath the shrouded hedge where
milk plashed, flowed, then spilled over
the pail's lip, voluminous.
Then she stole through night back up

to the dimming fire of her
shack, grinned toothless as dogs howled
the starlit valley alive,
some cold ember stoked bright-hot
in their brains, their sad language
lost to hill farmers' deep sleep.

That spring, those highland cows gave
no milk, their udders dry as
sleeves of droughted corn, and fields
in which they fell withered brown
and dust-dry, the season's rain
locked behind her smiling eyes.

The Farmer Who Loved Winter

He loved the killing frost that checked the sap,
that silenced the cicada's long debate. Even
springs and summers, when green

heaved him out to fields to work
from dark to dark, his small sleep bought
dreams of snow-cold ground,

dawn's December veil. Trains railed north
to colder countries, rolled from his county
through mountain towns till they hit taiga

yards, unpacked their frigid coal. And as he raked hay
from the barn's hot loft, his mind's slate of earth
was always bare, the fields gray, his wife's hair

spiced with conifer. When true winter
came, he walked his barren country, knew
darnel and thistle and naked wood were

merely stilled, the core pulsing its hidden life.
The hinge of the moon was cleansed and sharp
in bitter air. Stars wheeled round the farm.

No harm to him: Their salt shimmer
slaked his mind to know the soul's residuum
long out-glowed leaf or flesh, stem or stone,

returned to join and root in some new
flagrant spring, ghost-grown, abiding.

A Path through Walnut Trees after Rain

To be clothed in the smell,
a skin of sweet-rot, flowery,
life-dark as a pond floor—
their fruit felled, wet, fat,
half-black, half-green in slack grass
sugared in bees and calyx sap,
where blue squill and fern lift
to a bedraggled sun
from this pocked ground,
its mosses bright, this vanishing,
and later, starblown night.

A Study of Descent

Crabapple falls, flicked
by sun-strike and limb,
to patches of sphagnum
moss and twigs, right
into a cup of shale set slant—
then rolls, bruised,
to a bank of brown grass
where a creek speaks
its million silences.

From *April Creatures* (2014)

ജ

April Creatures

      1.

Today, nothing can keep me
                stepping from myself
through dawn's wolf-hued light dying
to thunder of coming storms.

Nothing can keep me
         from stepping ghostlike
into the boy I was, his story only half-told,
a voice for whom this wind was cipher,
this field of dallisgrass and spurge an open throat

toward utterance—

2.

Once, a boy
at pond's edge knew all mystery of light and water,
the limboid dark that cradled gar bones
and glass jars centuries old.

A woman's torn dress
gone gray, ragged, her hair still stitched to scalp like eel grass,
sunless, worm-cursed.

Wraith-self.

Around her, brass spectacles, a rusted ax,
cat teeth, a pouch of musket balls,

the pond-bottom
a chance cradle of ruin.

3.

The boy fled homeward along the spiderwort and calendula,
day's heat an ache in his legs, his bare feet
    quicker than the quickening scald of ivy.

Bees hovered, spun, sank again to green.
Ants swarmed back through their insatiate algebra.

    The pond now distant, a shimmering stain, silent,

        silent in the heat-waver.

4.

Nights, he lay bone-still in bed.

        Knew sorrow is not the blood-gloam pulse
        of the sun flaring
                  the low leaves. Knew sorrow
is partial to the undetectable,
        the unhoused chaos of every least life:

rotifer,
dinoflagellate,
amoeba:
                any protist swam and stopped
                through their staccato lives.

        No rhythm or sequence,
                        but languor
into which form falls: an oxbow
                rife with water moccasins,

        the wild that slake away
        their own dark bodies.

5.

Thus, sleep—

A dark country of yellow fields, a strawberry moon.
A sky blue as the underbelly of an indigo snake

and this dream:

Dusk's blue fingers struck the maples like matches
and beckoned him from the house's stifling fact,
the steaming kettle, red–burst asters

entombed in gray water, out to the open
meadow of his yard where under stars
brighter than the moon's own curse-light

he walked with peeled pears in pocket,
crossed the hissing creek, the clockless stone,
climbed the orchard fence to claim

a field of winter oxalis not his
to claim. As some near-ghost who'd long ago
singled out the door it must open

into death, he crept through
along the ice–lit meadow's edge, hedged into
a neighbor's lot, around the spectral

leaning shed, past ricks of kindling and frost–rimed
tools to find the stable's smells of chaff and dung,
the long white flare of the stallion's head.

6.

Any path you take is a path
                    of milk, of salt,
the cold shadow of bluebell wood.

If you cling to anything here—
            an obsidian shard, a leaf of smutgrass,
it will be taken from you
                    as dust.

This is where you end
and where you begin, where speech,

earth's only divination,
            scatters through the wind's
                    fixed lexicon.

7.

Flowering, the trees bend into their lives.
Insects rise. To adapt, birds collect
scraps, cast-offs, twigs and fallen feathers,

form them into whorls of warmth, where
mouths hatch from eggs to await
the worm, the crippled moth.

April bleeds stems,
seeds, the giant that unlocks winter's gray stone door,
casts into it unnumbered emeralds.

8.

The boy woke to the sound of foxes
screaming, left his bed to enter the vulpine dark.

No matter how many mornings
reversed for him, the sun's photons time-turning,
he always fell, a misstep
into stony fractures toward singularity.

9.

Those memories fade: the afternoon blasts four sparrows
to silhouette on their single swaying branch.
All shadows flutter.

Translucent, caterpillars bob in the wind
floating on green particles of all matter.

They cling to microfilaments delicate as air. Something
vital and black pulses through them.

10.

Sleepless, I hear the night
play its long, descending note.
If I close my eyes, figures robed in nebular dust come

and go through distant rages of light, opening
and closing their myriad doors.

11.

I cannot speak for all the emptiness
      between the earth and me,

    the cold spaces that hold this clarity.

    To lie down in winter grass,
        made hex, implacable.

    An omen branded
        into incorruptible meadows.

12.

Wasps seize the shed door then dip
to knotweed, cruel parabolas.
Demons squeezed into symbols

      to hum pain
      among the yard's stone coteries.

Yet the same gravities that lumber the sun,
      the moth, the word, drag them

down through spring rain
to thrash in clover, to amend
themselves to thunderous paper hells.

13.

Dogs bark at the sun-safe trees, where light
and shadow author act and meaning,

             green-heat and birdsong past all
praise and grief, motion, murder.

April carves through its brain again,
triggers its trillion ways to house a flower,

to sting and scorch with the fire
              of that cataclysmic star.

Under the River

Under the river, time is a dark fire, the earth
a mosaic of cellulose, silt, a few bubbling sloughs
where the sand floor gives way to blackish slime.

I have come to see what I cannot see: the land
tilting down to cold pocks of stone and sludge,
fallen trees that twine the water-path, a wooden

spine just under the drain of perception. Years back,
my father brought me here to fish. He helped me cast
the rod and watch the worm and weight sink down.

Trout plopped on our lines every minute or two,
and that night, he showed me how to slit jaw to tail
to let the vitals spill. Smoky trout hot off the fire.

Now when I step near the water, my father turns
away, for the light here forces clarity; the sun hangs
trees with swaying lanterns. Within the water

live a thousand thousand more rivers. The flow
wracks the stones with time. I turn away,
the river a ghost tacked behind my eyes.

The Day as Chapel

Not liturgy or hymn, venom or omen,
not books burdening the hands or flecks
of colored light traversing the preacher's brow
or priest's cheekbone, the pews of those who kneel to pray

their hearts to utterance, but rooms
of smoky light that house the myth,
that keep the breath in its holy amnion
and stagger the eyes through windows

to witness every molecule of green these pleas
manifest for noon and afternoon, till evening
plunders the underlands and seals every visible
star into its motion, every burning field.

The Longing for Western Distance

In the northmost tips of Carolina piedmont
distances are locked in leaves,
the open skies latched and weaved into yellow-poplar,
withe-rod and dog-hobble.
The dead heaps of slash pine near the gauzy lake
obstruct the eye.

I long for the red, bold brushstrokes
of Western plains, where the sun
douses ground, blends with rattlers and cattle
and the long white archipelagoes of cloud,
or the whole arc of our northern stars
spinning over desert, gorgeous as creek silver
cupped cold and dripping in rising hands.

From *Xylem & Heartwood* (2013)

ॐ

Fossil Creek

You were afraid of dying, hassled by dreams
   of drowning, the earth that turned
     you into dust. Sleep forced you to devour
      moonseed flowers until you seized, to sink

your head in a stagnant pond and witness
   your being flow away. What germ ran
     in those rooms, clogged your nights with fear?
      What hex hid in the attic's rot, the cellar's

Mason jars? Even dawns oozed despair.
   You'd wake in ghosts of sweat to gasp
     yourself alive. But even when you woke
      to sun, the pennant shadows hung

in corners, over bookshelves like a pall,
   even the fresh baked loaf of rye—they clung
     to walls, moved with morning's lambent arc
      into sunset to shutter dark the day.

You read in every dusk an eschatology, words
   from books long closed, pages burned
     and blown away. So out from the dark cage
      of that cloistral home into an open wood—

when you looked up to chart your pace,
   your eye battened to the sun for time,
     branches shattered sky, blue bottle glass
      or runes strewn to read your haunted face.

You walked the ridge and found a stream flanked
   in tongues of fern, plants old as any blood,
     bright as any pain. You lay among them
      where water rang the static stones,

where sapphire twigs of dragonflies flashed
   on leaves, blue syllables of words that rinsed
      your throat and brain. A language only water
         could know: cistern, leaf-meal, scatter, shale, phloem

xylem, burl, flow. Then, in the prone
   chapel of your skull glowed new weathers, some
      water-depth of consciousness, your spine a stem
         leaning toward that source that mirrored

your shared life, a life beyond the flesh, beyond
   your sewn mouth and sun-bleached eyes
      wherein your bones folded into that summer
         that always passes, earth's long, tireless tide.

Insomnia in Fall

In the gossamer notions between wakefulness
and sleep, when autumn dries your tongue like a leaf,
the clouds outside rise all scattershot and dim, unseen,
blood-hued over meadows of yellow grass.

With restlessness come the mind's worst specters:
a demon worm haunting the air, an old man who rocks
in the attic dark wearing a jacket of flame. You will
earth's creatures to heave the darkness back—

moths and sparrows become your heart's confidants,
bright as mica against the oak's black wood:
They speak to you in an idiom you understand
but never recall, then dim, disperse. A fish glows

in the pond outside. The pond an open mouth
from which the night pulls free slack words, says:
Here you turn with the leaves over an earth of spines
and jawbones. Let the stars latch your eyes.

From *Night Field Anecdote* (2011)

❧

Sweet Gums near Pond at Night

1.

Summer hauls away
its load
of storms, having dragged
its name again
through the gossip
of sudden rains.

I am still
sleepless, afraid to move,
as though what keeps me
awake breathes this solemn room
alive, grinning behind me
in the hackled dark.

As though a couple
gazes in through the window,
my insomnia the final answer
to their longing
for the afterlife, voices
flickering blue
in their open mouths.

2.

Now I can hear
the tall, sullen heads
of the sweet gums outside
lean into one another,
unlatching autumn
from its deep hiding.

The pond knows
to keep silent,
showing the world only itself,
its mouth full
of secrets closed.

3.

I want to hold
the answers
like the forest under the stars.
I want to lie down and rest, embroidered
into autumn's declension,
recalling nothing, no voice,

to know the blood
of the earth rushes over my skull
and trust it is music.

Trumpet Creeper

1.

June light comes again
and again without remorse:
Pollen rummages the blonde scalps
of spent deciduous hour after hour
until two sycamores puffed open by the wind bend
over the creek in twin green flames. Lacertilian armies
raze the garden and the yard's fringes,
flares for ruby-throats, bees.

Around the bowed trunks the loam shoots forth
lush feelers, sprung broad then clustered,
pink star-trails drooped at the stalk
and bursting
now to hum a song I almost hear.

॰ℭ

Coiled red mouths, they bloom beyond the shed
into unhinged greenness,
brighten, pump, swell through everything,
fall flaccid,
foiling their own morphology.

All spines suffer their histories, blossom-lattices
formed from water
in microfossil plumes,
when great black smokers
billowed up, kelp-like shifts,
fields of ducts, white worms, smokestacks—
a trillion trillion cellular divinities.

Preglacial, they shift into the woods and out again,
coil and articulate
deciduous nooks, flaunt the seasonal genesis:
vast gasps of light and air,
power of galaxies held forever in the lungs.

&

After June rain, I turn my back to the animals, the hush-
hush metaphors—abandon a green too brilliant
and face the black interstices of the tree-wall.

I feel the imminent collapse, the mass,
vibrissa crowding the ribcage,
my skeleton transformed under
the leaf-kiss, deep earth
watered down,
gourd unwrapped like a gift.

&

Heaven is neither lamb nor lion: Heaven
is symmetry's absence,
a trumpet creeper's seedpod
drained down the dead man's throat.

Strands and stalks expand
beyond order, uncontainable,
pierce thistle and stone:

Whittled to hair and bone,
the beast rolls its leaf-lobed head,
howls new identities.

2.

Summer sky an old onion.
Over the fence flares of pink trumpets.
Bees wheel about their coral bells, fly off.

      ↄ

I am meat, salt, water.
In my skull hums
a three-pound sentient chunk.
When I kiss my mother's hair,
a sleeping giant's heart blooms, collapses.

He shifts in his sleep and smiles,
mica flashing.

One day he'll look me in the eye.

      ↄ

A fleet of cumuli leans away.
Freighted with rain, bees drop
to the freshened grass,
red clover.

    3.

My great uncle Basil died when he was five years old
on a farmhouse floor in Iredell County, North Carolina,
half his face boiled from his skull.

Quilts and winter storms
broke my great-grandmother
to bone and a scorched gown,

pre-dawn dimness on a iron cauldron
that held the lye he tipped and spilled,
his little fingers charred,
hard as rust.

&

Sleeves of corn stalks flapped and clattered,
ash in the chimney flue, plum jelly's bright jar.

My grandfather turned in
his mother's darkness, eyes fusing.

&

As the calyx
unsheathes a petal,

as the hand holds
the scalded hand,

furled leaf,
heat to breathe and bear—

As water scars deep grain,
cottonmouths uncurl

over roots that twine kin
to smilax and larkspur:

the stream's clear coil.

The Potato

I wanted to be a potato, all brain and eyes,
born into the rhythm of worms, roots' suck
that throbbed me to life. When the field leaned

into fall, before the first frost reconfigured the sun,
I'd tremble in the hum of the hill's vegetable dark.
Sight clogged by clay, my nature saved from gravity,

I'd confound the apple, which drops abruptly
forever, bruised by limbs, the windfall flesh
sloughed into the yellow grass of my many throats.

I'd turn in a womb-furrow, a planetoid unhinged
from orbit. Above me a thick door would unbolt.
Plumped, warmed by the sun's annunciation,

I'd submit to the hunger of anyone who knocked
the earthen garments from my body, lifted me into air.

135

Ferns

Hard to trust the way they spin and nod in the light,
always looking away.

Older than the creeks they flank, their fossil tongues
fold to the sun in green, outstretched

syllables, asking their one question. When a body passes,
they turn and glare, eyes nested deep

in their black heads. Dense and sentient with more
history than the sweet gum that seeps

and falls, or ground water that diminishes
in the fattening sun, these reversed medusas

lick through stone, outstare all the locked houses
of blood and hair, outspeak

the millennial sky-clatter of bird language, leaf-litter
and lichen, reach out, take.

Prescribed Fire

Rain stirs clover and rot, rouses the beehive's thrum,
barn slats tiered in fungus. From bloodroot to cinder,
leaf-mold and cedar smoke bitter in six weeks' deepness.
Autumn deserves nothing it demands,
not ghost or doxology:

Say soon cinnamon and cider, soon scuppernong and gourd.
Years from now, the body disassembles; bees drowse
in their cells. Ash drifts through the field's red sumac,
spectral edge where two hounds guard
bright scraps of their kill.

No matter: A word rises the moment it is spoken.
Past fodder stacks and tobacco, near the small
blue vase on the sill, garlic crackles
and pales in a broth near-boil,
rain quells and the heart
owns its one room.

Creature Comfort

Even if loneliness sits on your eyelids nightly,
a skin of white fields and stone
skies your body refuses to shed—

know at least that the earth will remember
you, as you remember the corn snake
under your father's porch years ago,

how it curled up in the rotten wood
and dandelion like a red and white ribbon.
For days it lay motionless, the sun-glint

proving its eyes unendurably clear, alive,
the heat in that light keeping it still.
Know at least that one night, the grass bowed

as the snake slackened loose the crisp ghost
of itself, uncoiled its torsional radiance
and passed into the dark.

Rabid Cat

Rags of cheek sagged from the jawbone's white.
The sick mouth snarled, pocked throat
frothing half-rattle, half-growl.
When it dragged death's pong along the yard,
my father rigged a trap of chicken, wire,
and a stone meant to break its scabrous back,
which worked: Since madness shook the squirrel heart
in its gut, the gnawed mouth brave
enough to clink the latch trigger.
As if the bludgeon wasn't plenty,
my father aimed the gun and sprayed
the cat red onto the porch-wall.

Into morning, with gloves, bleach, and scalding soap-water,
we crouched into that pale gore, our sinuses torched
raw, hair steam-wilted, scooping jelly remnants into bags.
Pre-dawn lit the bed I'd lie sleepless in, that demon
eyeing my dream's door, and my father, dog-tired,
would heft the skull bits to the trees.

Chernobyl Eclogue

Day

Guards nod our white van toward Pripyat's yellow prairie, where
refuseniks hunker in robin's-egg-blue sheds. Peat-smoke
coughs from chimneys. "That smoke makes
plutonium," I say, and Sasha answers
"Da," almost too soft to hear.

Sasha is contaminated. We ride to his district,
tall grasses iridescent, swath of weak sun
peeling more than bark from birch. "It's the little
things," he says, though the forest
that's overtaken the carnival,

bleached of color, first catches my eyes. I know I won't
remember this: It's the sort of forgetfulness
the day demands: Sky's milky iris
dragging the afternoon, light
like a snapped bone.

Strontium roots deeper in his teeth when he speaks.
Licks his lips: "Old mother will say: 'We've survived
two bouts of starvation, and now
something invisible will kill us?
We'll stay here.'"

In the middle distance, her husband steps out from the fence,
his legs wrapped in pig hide below the knees.
He smiles, toothless, and as we close in,
I see the Holsteins, the harnesses.
The man's white eyes.

Inside—mushrooms. The couple has spent the day at harvest,
cooked these brown ribs cored with cesium,
wet with steam. They smell like rye but taste

140

of the autumn floor, rills spiced
with leaf-mold and rain.

At dusk, my head feels like a gourd in which the day
rattles. The sheds swarm and puddle with laughs,
and a little girl, her shaved head like a stubble
of gray corn, trails her soiled dress
through mud-slick grass.

Night

Window's rust-light. I won't remember it: memory
like groundwater radiates to weeds that jag
a shrew's belly, a hill-wolf that keeps its mouth

closed. Distant lumber truck huffs to Belarus.
And these small rooms, hot with stubbornness,
hot with some soft poison that leaks between them.

Sasha lies down next to me, his bare spine blanched
almonds in the moonlight. Behind the paper wall,
the fire snaps its half-life out to new snow.

Blonde Mare, Iredell County, North Carolina, 1870–1896

No one thinks of you anymore, your bones now broken
beneath the barn's dark rutted boards, turning
with coal, grass, and stars, those few deathless sovereigns.

Who witnessed you blossoming from the stable's
downslant of light, those mounds of golden hay
and chaff your grainy world until the fields lay open?

They worked you hard, your muscles hauling Scots plow
through furrow, chisel, and coulter loosening earth
till dusk. They'd prod you and you'd chuff.

But now they are with you, too, all knitted by death's
twine, your crux not lost but heaved by creek
and meadow, sluiced through the blowing manes of trees.

Family Portrait, 1790

North Carolina Blue Ridge

Here earth juts and tumbles in woods
where mountain creeks purl, slake through
rock, sluice schist coves and sheltered

gaps, then push hard through piebald sheer,
down to the slant of a cabin leaning:
Dusk's long shadow flickers dark

in this single room, where my kin
huddle around bacon that snaps,
burns over the fire's pine roar—

Fire grinds the weight of nightfall
on their silence, toil-dark scowls
over tight frowns, throats hungry

to down day's reaping. Here, land
is the sole tongue, etched in intricate syntax
of apple and trillium, the garden's blood idiom,

husk-dry stanzas quenched by prophecies
of rain. Nights, when their worn-out bodies
die into sleep, their dreams ration

to applewood and rattlers, valley's tobacco
and silage, the few words passed
down that I take with me, write, move on.

Peach Trees, Suffused with Pesticides

Hummingbirds stop
to bathe in the creases of leaves
where each least grass spider
has left the husk of its body.
The body ravels in the throat

when ends of limbs tremble, unlatch their petals
to a distant sea of hands:

the body
cannot scrub it out, this lack
of stain, emptiness gathering.

Burning House

Even though you only remember a pewter spoon,
the sap-dark core of oak and your mother's long shadow
snapping the screen door,

the ax strikes the wood's black heart:
You haul and stack racks of ruined cedar, ember
of the kitchen window across the blackberry and ice,

suffer the fox hour down the hill to suppers
of hot cabbage and salt and water, parsley and rye—
Even when the house smolders, crossbeams

hissing and finding their own charred context,
you step into the May-rush of another fire,
another room that spins and seethes.

The whole field, a sleeve of smoke.
Behind the wall, vermiculate hands,
the dusk's spring river.

Teleology: Recurring Dream

1.

If the door opens into an oak grove,
an intense greenness sentient with sun

and wind, avoid predication: with your eyes
masked by your hands,

say: *Our brains are storms*
over this dark river.

2.

If you venture into the cold smell
of stone, recent rain on slate,

or witness spars of elderberry
and jasmine's parched knot,

admit: *The moon is a requiem,*
its bone-pile light another entrance.

3.

What you carry, carry.
Put down what you put down.

If you fail to close the door behind you,
how will you acknowledge the world

without distraction? How will you
know that, even in dead

silence, a sound hums the cells?

Blue Pear

He lies reed-like in his bed as in his mind,
a lure to ghosts and master
of measuring light,

understands how the moon
finds under the elm leaves
just beyond the window

a raccoon's carcass, its mouth
and intestines ulcerated and sloughed
to runnels. A blue pear

lifted from a bowl. Minnows
prodding rain-scalloped shores, each spine
anchored for the moment's purpose.

He knows the elm is a cathedral
through which crows shake
and bend dark rafters,

leaf-light patinas on the far wall.
What is the music that falls on the grass,
retreats into the shuttered dark?

The man singing at the house's far end,
his mind a halved blue pear.

White Fox

She knows the fox's smell: ice and moldering apple,
the smallest contours of his mask—

She discerns the world as a slanted slate of white,
the smallest fracture, movement:

snake's arc in bayberry, the urn of a mouse's bones
picked clean. And as the fields outside

fall upward into snow, she sees how night shackles
her body, bright and plausible,

a mammal warmth, a vase of milk. When she tastes
his breath, all earth and fur,

an orchard afire, she knows the white fox has come
to sleep in the garden of her

mind, now bodiless, torn
leaf on stone.

Loggerhead Shrike

Trapped between sleep and wakefulness,
      mind perched in the high rafter, she sees
the shale tuft of its wing flared under night's
      shimmering arbor, the delicate articulations

of its kill: Out near the pond's muddy mirage,
      the shrike impales its shrew on a barbed-wire fence
and twists, empties that small cup of bones.
      Between earth and star, water and vacuum,

high clouds glow, the world's arc folds distances
      between Asia and her right iris, the eyes that won't
close, raveling the story her brain demands told—
      night's red omen a shadow on the wall.

Wolf Spider

Three nights in succession, the earth has pulled dawn
to the chapel, the first light-smear like a thorax split,
blood-arc, sky a spilled wound. Graves shimmer
like quartz on the hill, where ground craves
strong spring rain.

The chapel's windows toothed and gleaming. No one
knows why the yard's trees hiss hymns. No one knows
how the spiders, deep in hydrangea, seal behind
them calipers of space, stitch gossamer
bloom to bloom.

Thus, the heart moves to a warmer room, attuned
to April trees. Thus, the bee is caught in clouds
of filament, wrapped, gored, and eaten.
No matter: the leaf still increases
in the eaves.

The storm grows, spiders scatter, and bent grass
acquiesces to summer. When thunder riots
foliage, rattles the panes, holy relics gleam
blue on the altar. The night will always
swagger forth and fall.

Nocturne for the Second Death

At first, the wind sustains us, holds us aloft like gossamer:
the first sting of snow blown off dwarf pine
into towns that still constellate their fires,
dream and hoard the dimming myths.

To know the earth, we record expanse: meadow's longitude,
river's crux and the salt-sick coast. We search
farms of blighted corn, lean with their husks
to hear the underground streams snap

and sluice dry roots into the running. To know the earth,
we record microcosm: pine needle and paramecium,
pumpkin seeds rotting in hay. Always, when moths
raid the ruined factory and chew gowns to powder,
thronging the air with larvae,

one of us will stray: because the ice in her mouth is a lily
opening, because he leaves the purity of hunger
in a starved fox's stomach, lets maggots eat the gray eyes
to a dark scald. But we are forever assimilable,
even when the lights of the earth's curve

lock all the doors: We will wait centuries for the youngest
to boast and swagger in the silence he has become,
to stitch the sky as if he could bolster the light.
He returns as the last ember's hiss,
the last frost unsheathed.

Even spring, buried in water, we keep ourselves
down with the briar and bramble. When we can't bear to be
forgotten anymore, not by sludge or sleet, we unload
the bright syllables of our hair and skin,
then move on, torches in a tomb.

Ghost Water

We enter the pond during a night of glassy corners:
Frost toughens the grass, slows red oaks
until leaves unlock. The last minnows
like gray brushstrokes. We turn home
to see what's abandoned—

windowlight, Mason jars, blue corymbs of hydrangea,
fading like our skin that brushes past locust husks,
snake skins, old burdens shucked. Death smells
like wood smoke and clay, apple and ash,
thick as the slush our feet plume

near dank knuckles of water roots, mosquito eggs,
crane feathers trembling in shadows of bass.
Toads thrash the shore and plop into duckweed.
When we dive, the water sings away
the stories of our bodies,

our throats opened: grandmother's evening dress
drifts into the dark; grandfather opens his arms
in exaltation or dismay, all of us sinking below
circling gar and algal blooms
to where horse bones

shift in the slow pull, to the rich mud we take up
and eat, our mouths ripening,
white fire.

Winter Oaks

All night limbs hold
their blue lamplight aloft, ice
alive in the static understory.
I know how winter pulls the body

northward, makes the heart a cellar
in a sleepless house.
I know grass shatters
under that ossified eye. And just now,

when something moves in the mind
like a bluebird caught in an attic,
panicked, erratic, or descends
like the season's first snowfall,

I walk out to the oaks, bulbs
of my lungs shocked by the cold.
The night says: *Your breath unlocks the air with flowers.*
The night says: *Don't seek an easier way.*

From *Bledsoe* (2011)

ℰℭ

1. Behind the Brick Pits

Behind the brick pits
>   of Yancey County Waterworks,

Durant Bledsoe wobbles
>   out of sumac and bellwort,

grimaces pink-skinned
>   at how the world spins, swings

to the right. Hobbles along
>   the tree line from the braid

of sirens, the asphalt's linear
>   prophecy, forehead super-

heated and scathed in the sweeping
>   back and flay of limbs,

Gasping. Shame a char-smear
>   on his ear. Sweat begins to rinse

that filth away. Hemorrhage-hot,
>   dead center, the sun grinds

his muttering down to bare
>   declaration, whine and howl:

Ain't no need to warsh, Mama,
>   *when I seen your blood the while.*

Ain't no need to warsh
>   *when you're bald of mouth and eyes.*

Smells of smolder, choking
>   on panic with trees leaning in.

Mind-frayed, he turns to memory,
      images flashpoints of light

searing, the story unbolted
      and lucid, sparked by the flinty

dusk-kindling of insects. Car engines
      jeweled by distance, shining nearer.

10. Pulp of Dying Mountain Town, Its Remnant

Pulp of dying mountain town, its remnant
      rust-works, railway and mining deaths

cached by mycotrophic vines and barbed wire
      twining the pits, Blue Ridge pottery

toothed in clay. Wind a gasp of sorrel
      and stagnancy. Mountains: towering

monasteries of doubt. Chore of hog-slay,
      chop of ax head and helve,

disemboweling of liver, lights. Brains,
      gray matter scooped from skull.

Killed to live: killed after the blackberries,
      killed after the oak bore the blood-leaf's

prophesy, after winter's first frost.
      What was spring here but empty

remedy? Valley farm like a collapsed body.
      Here and there stands of winter oak.

Everywhere contagion that seethed
      up through sagged porches and musty

bedrooms blackening in corners. Resin-leaks.
      A mattress thin on box springs, quilt

under a cross to assure that spirit forsook
      the body. Kept minds locked tight

in the heartwood of myth. And Bledsoe's
      sleep deep without a pillow.

Beaten down into dream: The house
      filled up like a creek bed root-choked

the rooms spat out and left to fester.
      Where could a man run off to solitude,

break out of cellar-smother, air cached in
      jarred jelly and pipe-water: Past
                      pared to summary?

19. *What They Told Me*

What they told me is I don't
        have long. Something's grown

in my head and spread 'round
        to other parts. They want

to coop me up in a hospital
        up yonder in Knoxville.

I told'em I'd die at home. I won't
        have my spirit trapped up

in a strange city. He hauled her
        on his back after he got

the shawl on her shoulder,
        She clasped her arms

tight around his throat. You goin'
        to have to take me round to Crane's

so I can get them pills. He'll put it
        on our tab. Lord knows I hain't

got the money to pay'm nohow.
        Swung door back into heat

of the day, the sun high
        and bright. He stared

ahead, blood pounding fierce
        in his forehead. Swallowed.

I hain't goin' back to no doctor.
        I told'em you'd look after me.

After the pharmacy, he'd take
      one of two trails back home:

the first sheer, the second
      briar-strewn, neither easy.

20. In Middle Age, in Those First Leaf-Strains

In middle age, in those first leaf-strains
       and the smoke-tinct of winter, in the birdless day,

the memory becomes augural.
       An unearthed gospel, the story ends

before it begins, tale in fragments and strewn
       like shards at a man's feet. This fact

forced Bledsoe to tread north till small hills
       angled up and the pond on their land's rim

came into view. The church on its west end,
       hollow and crumbling on a berm of weeds.

Ain't supposed to be up here in the gloaming.
       He moved on anyway. Stripped his clothes

and walked into the water-grass, waded
       across to the cold center. Shivered.

Ain't supposed to be here in the water
       this time of day. Daddy said it was deeper'n most.

He'd imagined a train car lodged beneath
       the surface, red, rusting, and lined

with bones of the trapped. Dreamed of gold
       treasure flashing down in the water weeds,

pearl strings and fish eggs stippling the mud.
       And the farm tools of his great-grandfather,

chaff-cutter and flail, scythe and plough
       half hidden in a century of rain.

Congregated, washed to fracture. His feet
      dangling over a universe forgotten. Ancientry.

Suddenly, he knew: knew by autumn cirrus blueing
      in the dark. By the wind-tip spilling a chill

on pine, cones plopping into shallows,
      the gar beneath him shocked from his frigid

heaven of muck. Water moccasins dragging
      the black pennants of their bodies beneath

the shale. And in dead center, him, a chalk god
      noctilucent in the violet air, who knew

the pond had become prayer, somewhere beyond throat
      and brain, beyond tongue and voice—

21. Dear God of the Dead-haunted

Dear God of the dead-haunted
       heart, this water streams

with night and stars. My mind
       a tinderbox, set to flare

from the fire your voice conveys.
       Faith a wooden pendulum—

this surface a door that gathers
       to take me in. God of my kin

and bind-weed bloom, glacier
       and chert, light darkens

within her, back there in
       the overrun meadow. Back

there in the house where I was
       born. My mind is the field

where cattle ribs inherit
       earth, stripped by vultures

and rain, where that house
       slants down into soil.

My body a shadowbox,
       a grave of silt. An aging

pine sheathed in resin,
       leaning away from the source

that helped it begin. Swarmed
       with buried incident. Piling

the days, gnawing them back,
        whittled down by those failed

purgations of grief. And no words
        left but the words I remember:

one is farewell. And though
        loneliness sits on my eyelids

nightly, I know at least the earth
        will remember me, this body

your decoding of stone, star, nebula,
        the axis of the moon locked,

this world a kingdom of weeds.
        The horizon shimmers, the tipped

strata of leaf-way, cloud, and question—
        God, seeped in cells of wind-

fall apples, bee-burrows
        drunk on the hymns

of excess, singing the hours
        to barns and fences, singing

the sweet smoke above
        the tree line, far-distant,

hedged by the cold wind
        that descends to greet it,

God, have I only to tarry
        here? Have to turn

with the earth bearing little
        more than the pure

knowledge of the unborn,
        my voice sewn shut, burned

by this valley? If water
        were death's kingdom,

if this small, off-set yawn
        of pond the way to drown

down into paradise,
        then help me break

through the worms' domain.
        Let my shadow enter.

28. To Wash Her. Up in the Dank Room, Her Body

To wash her, up in the dank room, her body
      sketched in the heat. He brought the sponge

and scalding soap-water, woke her, helped
      her sit on the bed's edge. Wheezing. Face

mostly teeth and pits. Pain with every heartbeat.
      He gently touched her face. Smells of sweat

and sweet rot. Body giving away to bone. Blood on bed,
      midway down. Time to warsh, Durant?

I 'spect it is, boy. Wait that I catch my breath. An' go fetch
      us a clean cloth along with that sponge.

Outside, strict downwardness—rain pelted the bent
      grass, black branch flickered in the flash.

His mother bone-cold, bone-fevered
      in her own generous storm,

sea-surge of atoms fast to seep
      organs with waste. Earth's dark talent,

body's cells in aspiration. To wash her. After he
      rinsed her neck and back and tucked her again

into her ache, the post-rain creek raged
      with flux, called birds to tentative praise—

Thus her body's din attuned with April trees,
      dread lit by her mind that softly turned to song.

29. *She Slept in Fits and Fever*

She slept in fits and fever
      with an eerie smile,

convinced down deep in
      the white-hot realm

of ill-fed delusion
      that two gray faces

of the sparrow lived
      among her kin.

Sparrow east, sparrow
      west. Most times birds,

but sometimes they's old
      women. Old and wiry

and hacking up dust. Lord,
      but kind. They'd a-brung me

anything: firewood, good
      'maters in the dead

of February, a killed, cleaned
      deer. They'd a-brung me

the moon if I'd asked.
      Her mind an attic

where the chimney passed
      through. Where dust,

ash, and sparrows
      settled hard and nodal

in the corpus callosum.
        Lord I 'member one time

my daddy got up, hollered
        and blasted them possums

plum from the porch in dark
        morning. When I woke

to the yard I saw that kyarn
        hard and unashamed

in first sun. The ol' farm mutt
        nursed a maggot-hole deep

as an eye socket in the bulged
        back of the biggest'un.

Like a little bone-thatched cove.
        Like a grin a-blood. We didn't

et the meat, though we needed it.
        And I 'member that little box

of churchlight yonder where
        Durant and I'd a-sing

in tongues. He'd get afeared
        and I'd have to stop half

through spells and fetch him
        home. He'd be a-weepin'

constant. Memory's door gave
        way to worse fever, heat

like an open oven. Oh, Lord,
        there's those sparrows in

the basement. She convulsed in
        her vision of ash-gray birds

preening in the cellar's
        vegetable dimness, mold

like religion spreading
        into the least cranny

deep into wooden joists,
        up through rust-grazed

pipework and yellow
        rat bones, walls' relics.

Lord, them two sparrows'll be
        anywhere I want'em.

Sisters under my own skin.
        Her forehead gushing.

Mouth dry, a socket. Eyes
        squinting into a light

that wasn't there. I 'spect
        I need y'all to bring me

some water and a rag
        to wet my eyes. The roof

above her now cloud,
        letting in wind and rain.

30. Then the World to Black

Then the world to black.
       She still dreamed of green

lawns, minnows, hickory-horned
       devil moths. But dark rings

around the pictures: A haze of gnats
       rimmed the woods, goats and rye

on the wind. Winter rolled on
       to flower, a sweep of bright

cells. No matter: The field
       shrieked into grief. Hour

of thorns, the stone cutter's
       chisel. Go ahead and let the world

                  return to dust.

31. *Time to Leave You*

Time to leave you, boy, I'd suture you to me
      if I could. Closed her eyes: Cancer

crawled in her like spiderlings
      hatched from withered sacs

of her lungs, Walked wincing.
      From her bed the salve-smell

sweat on sheets: always around
      him. The ache, always: She begged

and begged, nightly now—
      Boy, all I ask is a smother

in my sleep. Curl up some hemlock
      in my tea. Out. He needing

out from the blunt weight of her smock
      as she sat at dinner, forking

the bread, eating nothing. Durant,
      you hain't got no sense to know I suffer.

You hain't got a mind to do nothing.
      Land's feculence suffocating him

in its shoveled-over residue. Her breath
      like leaf-rot, apples set to blister in

the August sear. Take no mind
      of the molder. Turn your head away.

32. *In the Keening House, in the Night's Arc*

In the keening house, in the night's arc
     over her coughing fits and pleadings,

he stargazes from his pallet.
     A rush of living dark tears through

the country air, through the tall grasses,
     shakes loose over the sternum. To share

the panic of fleeing creatures—
     The awful fact of leaving her

dead and cooling in the house. No matter
     how far his flight, her body would mound

under quilts, her flesh would swell
     blue in the room whorled with stench.

So with a flick of a flame,
     there it would go.

33. Went.

Went. Crossbeams
        seethed and cracked

the end. The farm's
        old bones unlatched

a tall blaze, dawn behind
        a cloud of gasoline.

34. Dusk Comes, Heat Stays, Still

Dusk comes, heat stays, still
        douses his hair in salt, sweat.

Lost, lulled by dark, Bledsoe misreads
        the far hound's yowl as lullaby.

He limps on down to the stream
        bank, briar lashes needling

chiggers on his skin. Down further
        to the tick-leafed, scallop-prongs

of the sand-slews, rushes and snarl
        of water full of musk-smell,

cottonmouths folding their bodies
        deeper under, spring's bulls

and peepers terror-plopping.
        He washes scalp, face,

blood and cinder away and gone.
        Then, cooled, props his head

against the berm and ponders on
        her teeth, gnashed in

the death-frown, her eyes astonished
        and rolled-back white.

Bites down gently on his tongue,
        sleeps.

35. A Blackness Amplified, Greenness Insinuated

A blackness amplified, greenness insinuated:
      Insects chisel the night to a point. Summer

clouds bear no star. Beyond the tangle of limbs
      and detritus of a thousand falls, out east

toward the farms and the clearing, the house
      lies in a pile of smolder. What seeps

into the brain's dark apertures? What ignites
      the night's grammar or douses it silent,

something sheer and simple, quartz-glow?
      Sepal-green, the earth's rejuvenating

pain. Suddenly, a man lies down
      in his guilt and asks: Are you the lattice

or the bloom? Answers come as platitudes,
      tricks of dead light, peripheral. Thus sleep

forces signs, trespass, yellow dust in the throat.
      Summer turns quick yet heavy-footed

more potent than the fever
      that bleeds through him like a flower.

36. *Something Deep in Bledsoe's Vitals*

Something deep in Bledsoe's vitals
     strikes violent, itch turned pain

turned mania, clot in neck-vein
     and thalamus twinge. Heat holiness.

Body slumps, simply still
     in the climbing scald of morning.

37. They Find Him Near Noon

They find him near noon,
       the law's dogs set crazed on the reek.

Even as they haul him away,
       looking for the right cage for him

to wither in, his mind lies
       distant, radiant. Trees blossom,

lean away, give him
       room. Eyes scoured, his face

calcified, a coin set gleaming
       in the closing vault of days.

From *Dark Orchard* (2005)

৪০

Dreaming of My Parents

They are in a hotel somewhere
in France. The room smells
of ancient books. A hickory tree
taps against a window
where light pours golden,
as in Vermeer. How beautiful
they are, together again.

I cannot believe
his delight in smoothing
her hair with an ivory comb,
the strokes meticulous, delicate,
as if she were
a fragile doll cherished
through centuries.

Taking his feet
as if they were wingless
birds, she caresses them, lowers them
into steaming soap-water,
washes them with a touch so focused
that I have no choice
but to witness.

Night, Yonce's Field

I am in South Carolina,
fixed in a cathedral of flowers.
O Lord,
the night roads
snake these coldest fields:

All the girls I've loved
sleep warmly
in the foxfire of dreams,
married, raced off
toward oblivion. God,

if I am to be
a stranger keen
to any ripe word's madness,
then blend deep autumns
in my hands.